Kindergarten Connections

by Patty Claycomb and Annalisa McMorrow
illustrated by Marilynn Barr

About the authors: Patty Claycomb is an early childhood educator. Her books include *Animal Friends* (MM 2012), *Friends from Around the World* (MM 2013), and *Art from Throwaways* (MM 2014).

***

Annalisa McMorrow's books include *Holiday Crafts* (MM 935), *Save the Animals!* (MM 1964), *Love the Earth!* (MM 1965), *Learn to Recycle!* (MM 1966), *Sing a Song about Animals* (MM 1987), *Preschool Connections* (MM 1993), *Ladybug Ladybug* (MM 2015), *Twinkle, Twinkle* (MM 2016), *Rub-a-Dub-Dub* (MM 2017), *Incredible Insects!* (MM 2018), *Spectacular Space!* (MM 2019), and *Outstanding Oceans!* (MM 2020).

Publisher: Roberta Suid
Copy Editor: Carol Whiteley
Production and Design: Scott McMorrow
Educational Consultant: Shirley Ross

For a complete catalog, please write to the address below:
P.O. Box 1680, Palo Alto, California 94302

E-mail us at: MMBooks@aol.com
or visit our web site:
http://www.mondaymorningbooks.com

We welcome your feedback, suggestions, and comments.

1-57612-001-5

Printed in the United States of America

987654321

Introduction

A book of theme units, *Kindergarten Connections* is designed to take you through the school year, from the first day of class to the first day of summer vacation. Each chapter focuses on two themes and includes circle time, activities for letters and phonics, science projects, math rhymes and manipulatives, arts and crafts, and more. Reproducible patterns accompany many of the activities.

Incorporated into the themes in *Kindergarten Connections* are important skills and concepts for children to master. Children will work with various creative media (Art), explore the world around them (Science), discuss meaningful topics (Circle Time), encounter each letter of the alphabet (Phonics), become familiar with numbers and counting (Math), and strengthen their cooperation and memorization skills (Games). By interrelating these skills through unifying themes, you will make the activities come alive for every child in your class.

How to Use This Book

Here are some general hints to lead you through the sections of this book. Of course, your own instincts and experience—as well as your knowledge of the individual children in your classroom—should be your primary guide, but we hope these tips will help.

Circle Time

Use this time to introduce the themes of the month. Circle Time is the perfect opportunity for children to brainstorm, to share what they know about the given topics, and to ask any questions they might have.

A brainstorming session might go like this: Show the children a real leaf and ask, "What is this?" The children will say, "A leaf." Then ask, "Tell me some things you notice about the leaf." Lead the children to talk about its shape, edges, color, stem, veins, and so on, naming the things the children can describe but cannot name. To provide facts, say, "Let's talk about the veins in leaves. Where have you heard the word 'veins' before? We have veins that carry our blood throughout our bodies. What do you think the veins in leaves do for the plant?"

Circle Time is also an appropriate opportunity for reading suggested books, for hosting Show and Tell, or for introducing guest speakers.

Literature Links

To make a literature connection, read and discuss the suggested books that accompany many of the activities. These books were hand-chosen for their creative stories and art. Some are recognized classics, others are soon-to-be classics! Included for each is a description of the book and bibliographic information.

Phonics

Each phonics activity is accompanied by a large letter pattern to duplicate and give to each child. You can also enlarge these letters and post them in the classroom. The phonics activities are tied to the first theme in each chapter.

Science

The activities in this section provide hands-on opportunities for your class to explore some of the concepts and phenomena associated with the topics in each chapter. Whenever appropriate, we have included a box of science facts on the page. Relate these interesting facts to your students during circle time or at the beginning of the science projects.

Math

These activities include original rhymes, creative raps, and easy-to-learn chants that the children can repeat with you. Patterns for adorable, child-made manipulatives are provided for each math activity. Children can practice their counting skills by moving the math manipulatives on their desks as you recite the rhymes. Additionally, set and number cards are provided for hands-on recognition practice.

A "set" can be described to the children as a group of items that are alike. One way to introduce this concept is to bring out a handful of a specific item (such as buttons) and ask the children what the items are. They'll answer, "buttons." Then take a button, pencil, and crayon, and put them together. Ask, "Are these all alike?" The children will say, "No." Say, "You are right. This is not a set of things." Call the various items you use for counting (buttons, shells, counting bears, and so on) different "number sets."

Art

Currently, there is much debate among educators as to how much teachers should guide children's artistic experiences. Some feel children must have free reign to create and imagine without adult intervention, while others wish to offer more structure and supervision. The activities in this book will allow you to proceed in a way that's comfortable for you. Remember that process and product are *both* important and valuable.

Games

In a few chapters, patterns for concentration games are provided. Children love this game and will be able to use their memorization skills while learning more about the featured topics for each month. Other games include activities that feature counting and other math skills.

Chapter One
Fall and Colors

FALL MAGIC

• •

Materials:
White poster board, felt pen, glue, gold and red glitter, paintbrushes, small paper cups

Preparation:
Print the word "fall" on the sheet of poster board in large letters. Pour glue into small paper cups for groups of children to share. Mix gold glitter into half of the cups and red glitter into the remaining cups. Mix the glue and glitter well.

Directions:
1. Explain that during fall, many "magical" things occur.
2. Ask the children to brainstorm some of the things that happen in fall. To encourage answers, have the children act out the following suggestions:
• Flocks of birds flying
• Squirrels hunting for nuts to store
• Leaves falling
• Crisp breezes blowing, blowing, blowing!
3. Provide paintbrushes for children to use to dip into the "glitter glue."
4. Have the children work cooperatively to paint all around the word "fall," swirling their brushes like a fall breeze. The finished poster will look magical!

Extension:
Duplicate the Fall Pictures (pg. 9) for children to color, cut out, and glue to the Fall Magic poster. These pictures will remind children of fall's magic.

Literature Link:
• *The Stranger* by Chris Van Allsburg (Houghton Mifflin, 1986).
A stranger visits the Baileys' farm and brings with him an extended summer.

Fall Pictures

FALL FOOD CHAIN

. . . .

Materials:
Food Chain pattern (p. 11), colored construction paper (green, blue, black, and orange), crayons in matching colors, scissors, paste

Preparation:
Cut a strip of each color construction paper for each child. Duplicate a copy of the Food Chain pattern for each child.

Directions:
1. Explain the concept of a food chain: In a food chain, events happen in a special order. Point out the order on the pattern for children to follow. Have children color the leaf green, the river blue, the bug black, and the fish orange.
2. Explain that the leaf in the pattern is food for the bug, and the bug is food for the fish.
3. Give each child four strips of different-colored paper to make food chains. Have the children form circles with the strips and paste them together to form chains. The green should be the first circle, followed by the blue, black, and orange. The colors represent the same items that they did on the pattern.
4. Have children take turns explaining the food chain story with their chains. Encourage imaginative storytelling!

Literature Link:
• *Tunafish Sandwiches* by Patty Wolcott, illustrated by Hans Zander (Lippincott, 1975).
A simple food chain is explained using pictures and words that even very young children can understand.

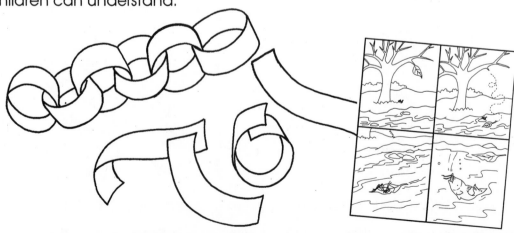

Food Chain Pattern

A leaf grows on a tree.   **The leaf falls into a stream.**

A bug eats the leaf.   **A fish eats the bug.**

SEASON MIX-UP

Materials:
White poster board, scissors, felt pen

Preparation:
Cut the poster board into four 12" x 4" rectangles. Print the name of one of the four seasons on each rectangle.

Directions:
1. Explain that fall is also called autumn. Then teach the children the Seasons Chant (below). Clap your hands to establish a rhythm. As you repeat the third line, clap slower to gently waken spring.

> **Seasons Chant**
> *School begins in autumn,*
> *Winter follows fast,*
> *Spring awakens slowly,*
> *Summer rolls in last.*

2. Choose four children to represent the four seasons. These children can stand in front of the rest of the class.
3. Give each child one of the rectangles to hold. The first child should hold the rectangle with the word "autumn."
4. Repeat the chant. Point to the children holding the names of the seasons as you name each one.
5. Have the audience yell, "Mix up!" Then have the four children change their positions. See if anyone in the audience can find the word "autumn." This child can move the "autumn person" to his or her original position.
6. Repeat the game often. It will reinforce the names of the four seasons, the way they are spelled, and the order in which they occur.

Literature Link:
• *Apples and Pumpkins* by Anne Rockwell, pictures by Lizzy Rockwell (Macmillan, 1989).
This rhyming story is illustrated in autumn colors.

THE DOUBLE "A" RHYME

· ·

Materials & Preparation:

None

Directions:

1. Explain that the letter "a" is a vowel. It has different sounds, including the short "a" sound in "pat" and the long "a" sound in "pay."
2. Ask for a volunteer to make two different sounds using his or her voice. The sounds can be silly, scary, or very quiet.
3. Teach children the fanciful Double "A" Rhyme (below).

> ### Double "A" Rhyme
> *A squirrel found an acorn,*
> *The acorn rolled away.*
> *But then he found an apple farm,*
> *And thinking that there was no harm,*
> *He loaded some apples into his car,*
> *And happily drove away!*

4. Reinforce the "a" sounds by going over the rhyme.

Literature Link:

• *Squirrels* by Brian Wildsmith (Franklin Watts, 1975).
This informative picture book has adorable, colorful illustrations.

Aa Patterns

THE BIG BROWN BEAR

· ·

Materials:
Bear patterns (p. 16), white poster board, felt pen, brown and black crayons or markers, Popsicle stick, scissors, glue

Preparation:
Print The Big Brown Bear Poem on the poster board. Secure it low on a wall. Duplicate the Bear patterns for each child and make one copy for yourself. Cut one bear out and glue it to a Popsicle stick.

Directions:
1. Demonstrate the sound of the letter "b."
2. Have each child think of a word that begins with the letter "b" to share with the class.
3. Teach the children The Big Brown Bear Poem. Point to each word as you read it aloud. Use the Popsicle stick with the bear on the end as a pointer.

> **The Big Brown Bear Poem**
> *B is for bear,*
> *A big brown bear—*
> *A burly bear, with big, brown paws,*
> *And big black claws.*
> *B is for big, brown bear.*
>
> *B is for baby bear,*
> *A baby bear with baby paws*
> *And baby claws,*
> *B is for baby bear.*

B is for bear...

4. Have the children color their bear pictures.
5. Post the pictures next to the poem.
6. When the children have learned the poem, ask for volunteers to stand by the bears, reciting the poem to describe the pictures.

Literature Link:
• *Big Black Bear* by Wong Herbert Yee (Houghton Mifflin, 1993).
This colorfully illustrated book is told entirely in rhyme.

Bear Patterns

Bb Patterns

COZY CATS

Materials:
Cat patterns (p. 19), crayons

Preparation:
Duplicate a copy of the Cat patterns for each child.

Directions:
1. Play a guessing game with the letter "c." Demonstrate the hard "c" sound and explain that a certain animal starts with the hard "c."
2. Have children guess animal names until a child guesses "cat."
3. Teach children the Cozy Cats rhyme.

> **Cozy Cats**
> *Cozy cats curl up on mats.*
> *Cozy cats have silky fur.*
> *Cozy cats can sleep in hats!*
> *Cozy cats don't meow, they purr.*
>
> *Cozy cats have eyes so green.*
> *Cozy cats have soft, smooth paws.*
> *Cozy cats keep themselves clean.*
> *Cozy cats don't show their claws.*

4. Give each child a copy of the Cat patterns to color any way they'd like.
5. Post the completed cat pictures on a "Cozy Cats" bulletin board.

Literature Link:
• *Cat* by Juliet Clutton-Brock (Knopf, 1991).
This Eyewitness Book is filled with color photographs and amazing facts about domestic cats, kittens, cats in history, big cats, the first cats, and much more!

Cat Patterns

Cc Patterns

AUTUMN BEARS

Materials:
Bear Food patterns (p. 22), markers, scissors, small paper bags

Preparation:
Duplicate the Bear Food patterns for children to color and cut out.

Bear Facts:
- Bears eat as much as they can in autumn to prepare for winter.
- Bears can gain one pound a day in autumn.
- Extra layers of fat help the bears stay warm in the winter.

Directions:
1. Discuss the fact that bears hibernate during the winter. When a bear is ready to hibernate, it will look for a snug place to sleep.
2. Give children Bear Food patterns to color and cut out.
3. The children can place their patterns in the small paper bags.
4. Have the children form a circle on the rug and empty their bear food bags in the center of the circle. Encourage them to observe the variety of foods a bear can eat.
5. Have children gather their patterns up again and take the bear food home to remind them of the habits of autumn bears.

Literature Link:
- *Animals That Hibernate* by Larry Dane Brimner (Franklin Watts, 1991).
This factual book includes color photographs of many animals that hibernate, including bears.

Bear Food Patterns

WHAT'S A LEAF?

Materials:
A variety of leaves, Leaf patterns (p. 24), crayons

Preparation:
Collect a variety of leaves and bring them into the classroom. Duplicate a copy of the Leaf patterns for each child.

Leaf Facts:
- A leaf is part of a plant.
- Leaves are found on flowers, trees, bushes, and other types of plants.
- Veins in leaves carry water within the leaf.
- The leaf stalk holds the leaf toward the light.
- Leaves carry food to plants.
- Water travels from the tree roots up to the leaves through tiny tubes in the trunk.

Directions:
1. Discuss different facts about leaves.
2. Place the collected leaves on a low table for the children to examine. The children can observe whether the leaves feel rough or smooth, whether or not the leaves have a smell, whether the veins are visible, and if there are stalks on the leaves. Acknowledge all answers as valid.
3. Have children color the different-shaped leaves on the pattern. They can circle their favorite shapes.

Extension:
Take the children on a field trip to look at the trees in your area. Challenge them to find leaves that match the ones on the pattern.

Literature Link:
- *How Leaves Change* by Sylvia A. Johnson, photographs by Yuko Sato (Lerner Publications, 1986).
Filled with facts, this book is a great teacher resource.

Leaf Patterns

SEED SURPRISE

Materials:
Dried large white lima beans, glass jar, water

Preparation:
None

Seed Facts:
- If plants didn't produce seeds, new plants wouldn't grow.
- Seeds fall from plants (the way an acorn does from an oak), ride on winds, float on water, and are carried by animals and birds.

Directions:
1. Have each child slowly repeat the following statement: "Plants make seeds and seeds make plants."
2. Demonstrate how baby plants live inside seeds. Place a handful of seeds in a glass jar. Pour enough water into the jar to cover the seeds.
3. After two days, have the children observe the seeds. Ask the children if they think the seeds look any different—larger or smaller?
4. Carefully remove one of the seeds and pull it apart. Have the children look for a baby plant—a tiny stem with tiny leaves.

Extension:
Have children look for seeds in apples, oranges, cucumbers, watermelons, and strawberries. The children can compare the seeds in size, shape, location (whether the seeds are found on or in the food), and amount.

Literature Link:
- *Rolli* by Kohi Takihara (Picture Book Studio, 1988). Rolli is a seed who rolls and rolls until he finds his resting place. Then he becomes a flower.

ACORN MATH

. . . .

Materials:
Squirrel and Acorn patterns (p. 27), Squirrel Math Problems (pp. 28-29), crayons (brown and gray), scissors, envelopes (one per child)

Preparation:
Duplicate copies of the Squirrel and Acorn patterns and the Squirrel Math Problems for each child.

Directions:
1. Give each child a copy of the Squirrel and Acorn patterns to color and cut out. Have the children color the acorns brown and the squirrels gray.
2. Have the children place their Acorn patterns on one side of their desks and the Squirrels on the other.
3. Read the Squirrel Math Problems to the children. As you read the problems, the children can manipulate their patterns on their desks.
4. After you read each problem, ask the children how many acorns the squirrel has.
5. Children can take the patterns and rhymes home in envelopes for additional at-home practice.

Literature Link:
• *The Tremendous Tree Book* by Barbara Brenner and May Garelick, pictures by Fred Brenner (Caroline House, 1979).
This resource is filled with facts about trees, including "Acorn Trees."

Squirrel and Acorn Patterns

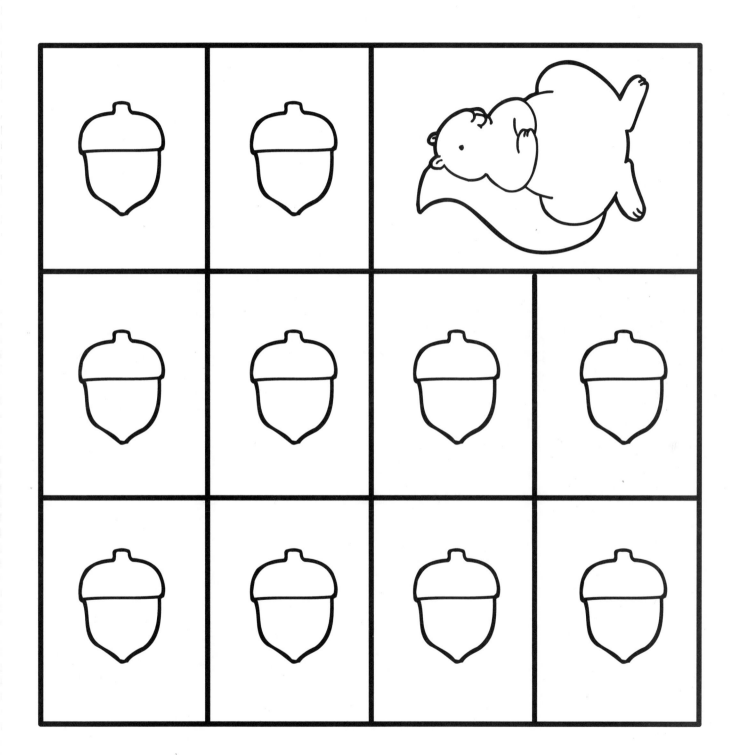

Squirrel Math Problems (1-5)

A little gray squirrel
Wanting some fun,
Picked a big acorn
And then he had . . . (one).

That cute little squirrel,
Just out of the blue,
Picked one more acorn
And then he had . . . (two).

The hungry gray squirrel
Climbed back up the tree.
He picked one more acorn
And then he had . . . (three).

The smart little squirrel,
He wanted some more.
He picked one more acorn
And then he had . . . (four).

That acrobat squirrel,
Deciding to dive
From the top of the tree,
Picked one more, and had . . . (five).

Squirrel Math Problems (5-10)

The squirrel and his buddy
Were out for some kicks.
They picked one more acorn
And then they had . . . (six).

That silly young squirrel
With his eyes up toward heaven,
Picked one more acorn
And then he had . . . (seven).

The loveable squirrel
With a very full plate,
Added an acorn
And then he had . . . (eight).

The squirrel and his sister
Decided to dine.
They picked one more acorn
And then they had . . . (nine).

The squirrel and his brother
They did it again,
They picked one last acorn
And then they had . . . (ten).

When nighttime had fallen
The squirrel went to bed,
And all through the night
Acorns danced in his head.
He knew that the sun would come up in the morn
And he and his friends
Would pick more acorns.

Acorn Number Sets

🌰	1	🌰🌰	2
🌰🌰🌰	3	🌰🌰🌰🌰	4
🌰🌰🌰🌰🌰	5	🌰🌰🌰🌰🌰🌰	6
🌰🌰🌰🌰🌰🌰🌰	7	🌰🌰🌰🌰🌰🌰🌰🌰	8
🌰🌰🌰🌰🌰🌰🌰🌰🌰	9	🌰🌰🌰🌰🌰🌰🌰🌰🌰🌰	10

WOOLYBEARS

. . . .

Materials:
Woolybear pattern (p. 32), glue, paintbrushes, paper plates, felt pens, brown and black tissue paper, scissors, white paper, tape

Preparation:
Duplicate one copy of the Woolybear pattern for each child. Cut tissue paper into small strips. Place glue on paper plates, making one plate for every two children to share.

Directions:
1. Explain that woolybear caterpillars search for bark and other places to hide under or in during cold winter weather.
2. Give each child a Woolybear pattern.
3. Show the children how to use the paintbrushes to spread glue inside the caterpillar outlines.
4. Provide tissue paper strips for the children to pinch into balls and glue to their caterpillars as "fur."
5. When the caterpillars have dried, tape them side by side in a row. Print the following message on white paper: "Woolybear caterpillars hide for the winter."

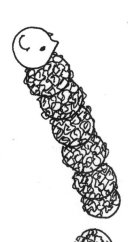

Literature Link:
• *The Very Hungry Caterpillar* by Eric Carle (Philomel, 1987). This classic story about a ravenous caterpillar continues to delight children more than 25 years after its original publication.

Woolybear Pattern

GLUE PAINTING

Materials:
White construction paper, glue bottles, paintbrushes, watercolor paint

Preparation:
None

Directions:
1. Have the children think of something that reminds them of fall, for example, trees, leaves, caterpillars, and so on.
2. Give each child a glue bottle and a sheet of construction paper.
3. Have the children use their glue bottles to draw outlines of autumn pictures.
4. Encourage children to add as much detail as possible. For example, they can make leaves with thick veins or frogs with puffy glue spots on their backs. The glue should be thick and high on the papers.
5. When the glue pictures have dried, the children can use watercolors to paint over their pictures.
6. Have the children share their glue pictures and explain why the images remind them of fall.

Literature Link:
• *I Am a Bunny* by Ole Risom, illustrated by Richard Scarry (Golden Press, 1963).
Nicholas is a bunny who lives in a hollow tree and watches the weather change. In each season, he has different favorite pastimes.

THE MAGIC FORMULA

Materials & Preparation:
None

Directions:
1. Explain that some leaves change color during the fall, and ask if any of the children has ever seen red, orange, or yellow leaves.
2. Discuss the fact that only certain trees have leaves that change color and drop. These are called deciduous trees. Have the children slowly repeat the word "deciduous."
3. Teach children the formula that turns leaves different colors:

> ### The Magic Formula
> *Chlorophyll makes green leaves bright.*
> *They stay that way from warm sunlight.*
> *But in the fall there is less sun.*
> *The leaves turn color, one by one.*
> *They change to red, then gold, then brown,*
> *Then they fall down onto the ground.*
> *But in the spring, just wait and see,*
> *All new green leaves will fill the tree.*

Literature Link:
• *Eyewitness Books: Tree* by David Burnie (Knopf, 1988).
This extremely informative book includes color photos of every part of a tree. It also features information on roots, bark, fruit, falling leaves, and more. The falling-leaf section is especially interesting.

TREE DROPS

Materials & Preparation:
None

Directions:
1. Have children brainstorm answers to the following question: "Why do some trees lose their leaves?" Remind them about the "Magic Formula" (p. 34). The answer involves sunshine. When there is less sunshine in autumn, leaves stop making the sugar that feeds the tree. The leaves then fall off the tree.
2. Have the children stand with their hands raised high. Repeat the following chant. At the end, have all the children drop their hands.

> ### Tree Drops
> *I am an autumn leaf.*
> *The air is cooler.*
> *There is less sunshine that shines on me.*
> *I can't make sugar for my autumn tree.*
> *So I slowly become red, yellow, and brown,*
> *And then very quietly*
> *I drop to the ground.*

3. Have the children pretend to be bare trees and stand with their "branches" (arms) sticking out.

Option:
Trace leaves onto colored construction paper using the Leaf patterns (p. 24) as templates. Give each child a paper leaf to hold while repeating the rhyme. Children can drop the leaves at the end of the rhyme.

Literature Link:
• *Leaves* by Fulvio Testa, English text by Naomi Lewis (Peter Bedrick Books, 1983).
This beautiful story is about a leaf remembering life in the tree.

AUTUMN WINDOW

. . . .

Materials:
White poster board, tape, felt pens (red, orange, yellow, green, and brown)

Preparation:
Draw a border around the poster board to create an autumn "window." Tape the window low on a wall. (For a larger window, tape two white pieces of poster board together, side by side.)

Directions:
1. Have the children brainstorm answers to the following question: "If you looked out a window in autumn, what do you think you might see?" Possible answers are: leaves on the ground, jack-o'-lanterns, apple trees, berries, and so on.
2. Ask for volunteers to draw a fall-related item in the window, using the felt pens that represent autumn colors.
3. When the window has been filled in with autumn items, ask for volunteers to tell you what they see out the window.
4. Make a sign above the window that reads, "What do you see through our autumn window?"

Option:
Duplicate the Fall Pictures (p. 9) for children to color using autumn-colored pens and then glue to the "window."

Literature Link:
• *The Cinnamon Hen's Autumn Day* by Sandra Dutton (Atheneum, 1988).
The Cinnamon Hen enjoys raking leaves in the cool autumn air, despite Mr. Rabbit's admonition.

THE RAINBOW FORMULA

Materials:
Shallow dish, small mirror, tape, two sheets of white paper, crayons in rainbow colors (red, orange, yellow, green, blue, indigo, violet)

Preparation:
Tape the two sheets of white paper side by side on a wall. Place the crayons on the rug near the paper.

Directions:
1. Have the children sit by the white paper. Explain that sunlight looks white, but it is made up of different colors. You can see the colors of sunlight when you see a rainbow!
2. Hold up the crayons one by one and repeat the color names.
3. Ask for seven volunteers to each draw on the white paper with one of the colors . (Help them to do this in the correct order of rainbow colors.)
4. Have children brainstorm answers to the following question: "Why can't you see the colors of sunlight all the time?" Answer: When light is "bent," it splits into the seven colors. Raindrops "bend" light.
5. Draw the rainbow formula on the remaining paper: The sun plus raindrops equal a rainbow! (The sun + raindrops = a rainbow!)
6. Do the following experiment when the sun is low in the sky and shining through a window. Place a shallow dish of water in the sunlight. Put a mirror in the water so it faces the sun. As the water "bends" the sunlight, a rainbow will appear on the ceiling!

Literature Link:
• *Skyfire* by Frank Asch (Simon and Schuster, 1984).
When a bear sees his first rainbow he thinks the sky is on fire!

WILDFLOWER WALK

Materials:
Wildflower patterns (p. 39), crayons

Preparation:
Duplicate the Wildflower patterns for each child.

Directions:
1. Have children brainstorm answers to the following question: "What is a wildflower?" Answer: A wildflower is a flower that grows untended. Wildflowers grow in the woods, in fields, along roads, by lakes, and many other places.
2. Give each child a copy of the three flower pictures.
3. Teach the children the names of the flowers. Point out that the flowers begin with the first three letters of the alphabet.
4. Have the children color the flowers and add grass, the sun, insects, animals, or other flowers!

Extension:
If possible, take children on a walk to look for wildflowers. Have children observe where the flowers grow and what colors they are. Have children look for flowers that grow in gardens, also. Ask if they can see any differences between the two types of flowers.

Literature Link:
• *Alphabet Garden* by Laura Jane Coats (Macmillan, 1993).
An alphabetical tour of items found in a garden, beginning with arbor and ending with zinnia.

Wildflower Patterns

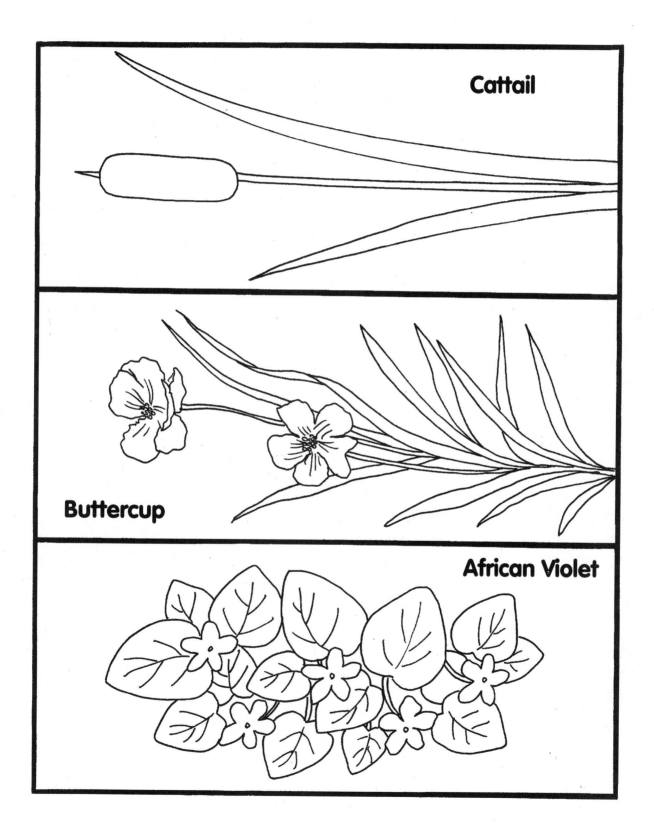

Cattail

Buttercup

African Violet

39

ANIMAL MAGIC

· ·

Materials:
Weasel pattern (p. 41), brown construction paper, pencils, scissors, tape

Preparation:
Duplicate a copy of the Weasel pattern for each child.

Directions:
1. Explain that some animals begin to change color as the colder winter months approach. For example, brightly colored birds can change to grays, browns, and dark greens during autumn. This helps them to blend in with their surroundings when the winter comes.
2. Weasels change color from brown to white. Ask the children the following question: "If you were a weasel in the snow, and an animal or a person was hunting you, would you rather be brown or white?" Have children give their reasons for their answers.
3. Give each child a copy of the Weasel pattern, a sheet of brown paper, and a pair of scissors.
4. Have the children cut out the weasel pictures and place their white weasel on their brown paper.
5. Demonstrate how to trace the weasel's outline onto the brown sheets of paper.
6. Have children tape their white weasel pattern directly over the brown outline. Show them how to place the tape near the top of the weasel's back.
7. Explain that now the white weasels are ready for winter. Children can peek under the white fur to see the brown fur—ready to grow when the warmer months arrive.

Literature Link:
• *Discovering Weasels* by Miranda MacQuitty, illustrated by Wendy Meadway (The Bookwright Press, 1989).
This nonfiction book is filled with interesting information about weasels and is illustrated with photographs as well as drawings.

Weasel Pattern

LEAF GRAPHING

Materials:
Leaf patterns (p. 24), Graph pattern (p. 43), colored construction paper (green, yellow, red), scissors, large paper bag, white poster board, tape, crayons (green, yellow, red)

Preparation:
Duplicate the Leaf patterns and cut out leaves from the three different colors of construction paper. Make sure that there are enough leaves for each child in the class to have at least one. Cut a different amount of leaves from each color of construction paper. Place the leaves in a bag. Duplicate and enlarge the Graph pattern; color one leaf red, one yellow, and one green; and tape the pattern on a wall.

Directions:
1. Have the children sit in a circle and dump the leaves in the center of the circle.
2. Have the children sort the leaves into piles by color.
3. Have each child tape one leaf under the appropriate column on the graph. If there are extras, volunteers can tape the remaining leaves in the appropriate columns.
4. Have the children observe the leaf columns. Ask the following questions: "Which color do we have the most of?" "Which color do we have the least of?" "Which color is in the middle?"

Option:
Collect a large variety of different-shaped leaves. Do this activity with real leaves that you collect from your playground or neighborhood. Make sure that you have some leaves from the same trees, in order to create a successful graph.

Literature Link:
• *Fresh Fall Leaves* by Betsy Franco, illustrated by Shari Halpern (Scholastic, 1994).
This 16-page book lists all sorts of fun things to do with fall leaves.

4 red leaves

Graph Pattern

THE APPLE ROLL

. . . .

Materials:
Bowl and Apple patterns (p. 45), crayons or markers (in red, green, and yellow), scissors, felt pen

Preparation:
Duplicate a copy of the Bowl and Apple patterns for each child.

Directions:
1. Give each child a copy of the Bowl and Apple patterns to color and cut out.
2. Have the children place five apples on top of the Bowl pattern.
3. Teach the children The Apple Roll Chant.

The Apple Roll Chant

Five little apples in the bowl,	(hold up five fingers)
One fell out and started to roll.	(rotate fists)
It bumped the table and hit my feet,	(clap hands)
How many apples left to eat?	(wave fists in the air)

---

4. Have the children move one apple off the bowl.
5. Ask the children to count the remaining apples and tell you how many are left.
6. Continue until all of the apples have rolled out of the bowl.
7. Ask the children how many are left. (zero)

Option:
Have the children color and cut out ten apples to use with the apple chant. Have the children choose how many apples roll out of the bowl at a time.

Literature Link:
• *An Apple Tree Throughout the Year* by Claudia Schnieper, photographs by Othmar Baumli (Carolrhoda, 1987).
This factual book includes many color photographs of apple trees and follows the stages of apples' growth, from flowers to fruit.

Bowl and Apple Patterns

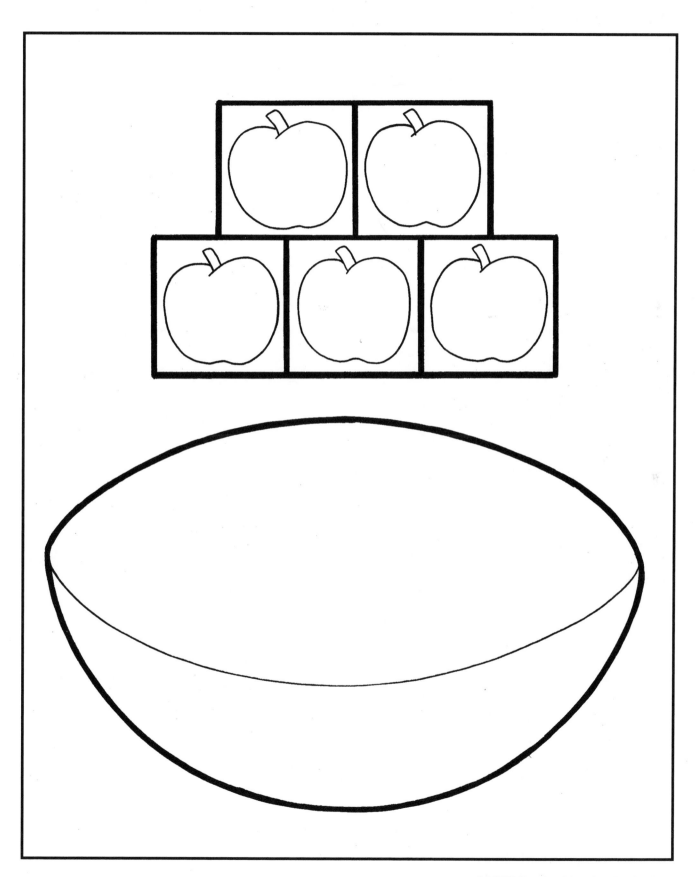

Apple Number Sets

🍎	1	🍎🍎	2
🍎🍎🍎	3	🍎🍎🍎🍎	4
🍎🍎🍎🍎🍎	5	🍎🍎🍎🍎🍎🍎	6
🍎🍎🍎🍎🍎🍎🍎	7	🍎🍎🍎🍎🍎🍎🍎🍎	8
🍎🍎🍎🍎🍎🍎🍎🍎🍎	9	🍎🍎🍎🍎🍎🍎🍎🍎🍎🍎	10

SPONGE IT

Materials:

Butcher paper, scissors, sponges, paintbrushes, tempera paint (brown, red, orange, yellow, and green), paper plates, white paper, tape

Preparation:

Cut one three-inch oval sponge for each child. Cut a two-foot-tall sheet of butcher paper for each child. Make paint palettes by squeezing small amounts of tempera paints (without mixing the colors) onto paper plates. Two or three children can share each palette.

Directions:

1. Give each child a sheet of paper, a sponge, and a paintbrush, and distribute the paint plates.
2. Have the children paint tree trunks and branches on their papers.
3. The children can add autumn leaves to their bare trees by dipping the sponges in the various paint colors and dabbing it on. (Tell the children not to worry if the paint becomes mixed on the plate or sponge. Autumn leaves are a pattern of different colors!)
4. When the autumn trees have dried, tape them side by side low on a wall. Take the children on a slow walk through their beautiful, wooded area.

Literature Link:

• *Once There Was a Tree* by Natalia Romanova (Dial, 1985). This beautifully illustrated book could serve as inspiration for children's tree paintings.

Colors
Art

AUTUMN SPRAY

. . . .

Materials:
Leaves (real or construction paper), glue, newspaper, white construction paper, spray paint (gold, yellow, and red), gold glitter (optional)

Preparation:
Collect leaves—at least six or eight for each child. Or duplicate the Leaf patterns (p. 24) and cut out six or eight construction-paper leaves for each child.

Directions:
1. Give each child a sheet of paper and a handful of leaves.
2. Have the children glue their leaves onto their papers.
3. When the leaf pictures have dried, take the papers outside and spread them out over large sheets of newspaper.
4. Spray paint the leaves using a variety of colors of paint. (Do this when the children are not present.)
5. Post the finished pictures.

Option:
Sprinkle gold glitter on the wet paint to add an extra sparkle of autumn color.

Literature Link:
• *Why Do Leaves Change Colors?* by Betsy Maestro, illustrated by Loretta Krupinski (HarperCollins, 1994).
This read-and-find-out science book explains how leaves change their colors in autumn.

Chapter Two
Halloween and
Things with Wings

HALLOWEEN MAGIC

. . . .

Materials:
Paper plates, Popsicle sticks, tape, black markers

Preparation:
None

Directions:
1. Explain that Halloween is a celebration in which children (and some adults, too) dress up for fun and receive treats or play tricks.
2. Encourage children to describe costumes they've worn in the past.
3. Have children make masks with paper plates and markers.
4. Demonstrate how to tape Popsicle stick handles to the masks.
5. Teach children the Halloween Magic rhyme. They can hold up their masks when masks are mentioned in the poem and yell "Trick or treat!" at the end of the rhyme.

> ### Halloween Magic
> *On Halloween, the children dress*
> *In costumes, wigs, and hats.*
> *They put on masks and makeup*
> *So they'll look like ghosts and bats!*
>
> *On Halloween, the children go*
> *Parading down the street.*
> *They ring the bell, put on their masks,*
> *And then yell, "Trick or treat!"*

Literature Link:
• *Strega Nona* by Tomie de Paola (Prentice-Hall, 1975).
When Strega Nona, a "Grandmother Witch," leaves Big Anthony in charge of her house, the excitement starts!

SUPER SPIDERS

· ·

Materials:
Spider pattern (p. 52), scissors, construction paper, crayons, marker, glue

Preparation:
Duplicate and enlarge the Spider pattern. Glue it to a piece of construction paper. Duplicate a copy of the Spider pattern for each child.

Directions:
1. Gather the children in a circle. Explain that spiders are helpful. They eat insects that bother humans.
2. Ask the children to tell you how they feel about spiders.
3. Display the enlarged Spider pattern. Have the children help you count the spider's legs and eyes.
4. Number each leg with the marker as the children count. Explain that while many spiders, like the spider in the picture, have eight eyes, some have only two, four, or six. All spiders have eight legs.
5. Provide crayons for children to use to color the Spider patterns.
6. Post the finished pictures on a "Super Spiders" bulletin board.
7. Teach children The Spider Poem. Clap to establish a rhythm.

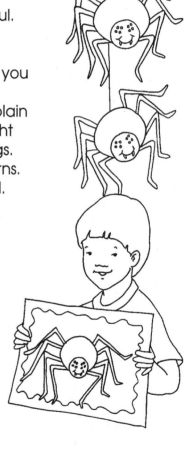

The Spider Poem
Spiders are not insects.
Spiders have eight legs.
Spiders have four pairs of eyes.
Spiders hatch from eggs!

Spider webs are sticky.
Spiders weave them tight.
Spiders spin that silky string.
Spiders weave webs right.

Literature Link:
• *Spiders Near and Far* by Jennifer Owings Dewey (Dutton, 1993).
This factual spider resource has many beautifully illustrated pictures.

Spider Pattern

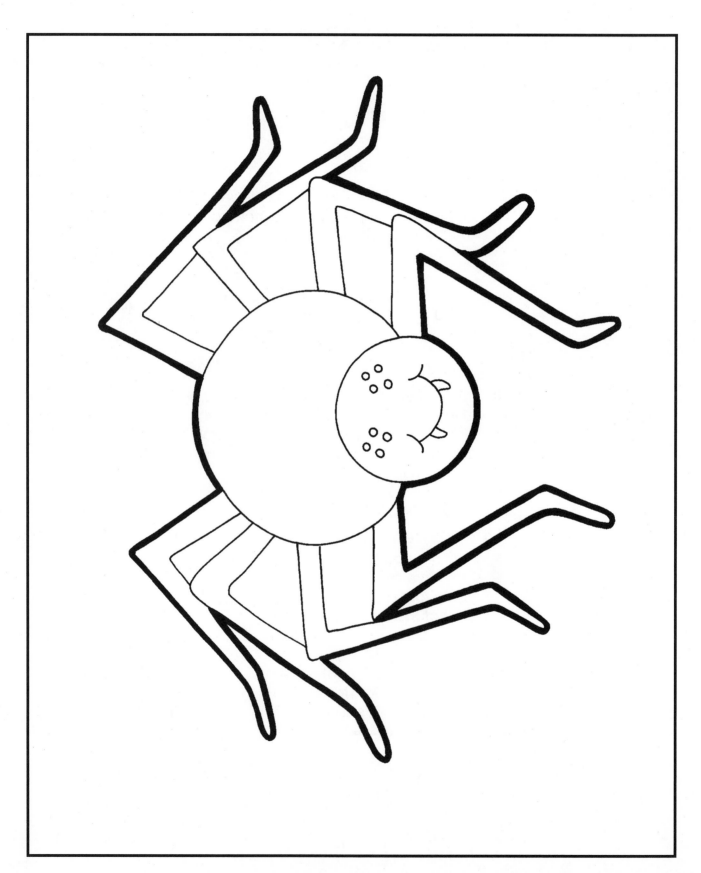

THE TRICK OR TREAT "D" RIDDLE

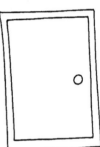

Materials:
Starts with "D" patterns (p. 54), crayons, scissors, flannel board, flannel, glue

Preparation:
Use a rectangular flannel board as a door. Cut a circle from flannel to serve as a doorknob. Duplicate the Starts with "D" patterns, color, and cut them out. Glue a piece of flannel to the back of each pattern. This will make the patterns adhere to the door.

Directions:
1. Demonstrate the sound of the letter "d." Have the children repeat the following sentence and listen for the words that begin with "d." Speak slowly as you say, "One dark and dreary night, I heard a knock upon my door."
2. Set up the flannel board door, keeping the patterns hidden.
3. Have the children pretend that it's Halloween night and the people knocking on the door are children dressed in disguises.
4. Teach the children the Trick or Treat Chant. Pound one fist against your palm as you say, "Knock, knock!" Clap as you say the rest of the chant.

Trick or Treat Chant

Knock, knock,
Trick or treat,
Knock, then knock some more.

Knock, knock,
Trick or treat,
Let's see who's at the door!

---

5. Pull out the first flannel board pattern and stick it on the door.
6. Have the children call out the name of the disguise.
7. Repeat the chant with the children, then add the second "d" pattern to the door. Continue until all patterns have been placed.

Literature Link:
• *Trick or Treat, Danny!* by Edith Kunhardt (Greenwillow, 1988).
Danny is sick, but his friends visit him on Halloween to cheer him up.

Starts with "D" Patterns

Dragonfly

Dog

Dragon

Duck

Doctor

Dinosaur

Dd Patterns

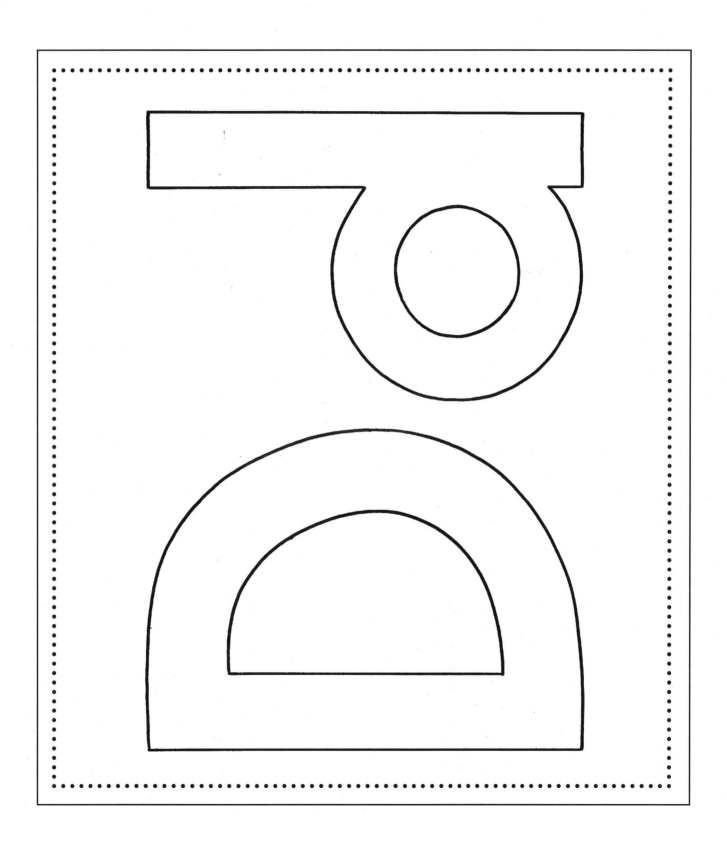

Halloween
Phonics

EEEEEEK!

. . . .

Materials:
Mouse pattern (p. 57), white construction paper squares (one per child), scissors, felt pens (black, orange, and gray), tape

Preparation:
On each paper square but one, print the letter "e" using the black and orange felt pens. Write the letter "k" on the remaining square. Hide the letter squares around the room. Duplicate the Mouse pattern, color it gray, and cut it out.

Directions:
1. Have the children repeat the long sound of the letter "e," then search the room for the letter squares.
2. Tape the squares in a row on a wall with the "k" at the end.
3. Sound out the word "Eeeeeek!" with the children.
4. Tell The Scary Halloween Story. Have the children say "Eeeeeek" when you point to the word.

> ### The Scary Halloween Story
> *Once there was a boy who was afraid of Halloween. He thought that on Halloween he would see something scary and he would yell, "Eeeeeek!"*
>
> *On Halloween, a group of trick-or-treaters knocked on his door. Slowly, he opened the door. On his step stood a ghost and a goblin. The little boy wasn't scared at all. Nearby stood a robot and a black cat. The little boy wasn't scared of them, either.*
>
> *But then the little boy saw something else and he screamed "Eeeeeek!" Why did he scream?*

5. Tape the mouse picture on the wall and read the entire line: "Eeeeeek! A mouse!" The little boy was afraid of the mouse!

Literature Link:
• *The Mouse's Terrible Halloween* by True Kelley (Lothrop, 1980). Halloween brings further misadventures to the Mouse family.

MONSTER FUN

. . . .

Materials:
"F" Monster Parts (p. 59), construction paper, scissors, glue, crayons

Preparation:
Duplicate a copy of the "F" Monster Parts for each child.

Directions:
1. Have the children repeat the sound of the letter "f."
2. Explain that the children will be making monsters using patterns that start with the letter "f."
3. Give each child a set of patterns to color and cut out. Have the children say the names of the monster parts as they cut them out. Discuss the descriptive words that start with the letter "f."
4. Have the children draw their own monster pictures, then glue the "f" patterns to their pictures.
5. Post the completed monster pictures on a "Funny, Friendly, Fearsome Monsters" bulletin board.

Literature Link:
• *You're the Scaredy-Cat* by Mercer Mayer (Parents' Magazine Press, 1974).
Two brothers camp in the backyard. One scares himself by telling a monstrous story!

"F" Monster Parts

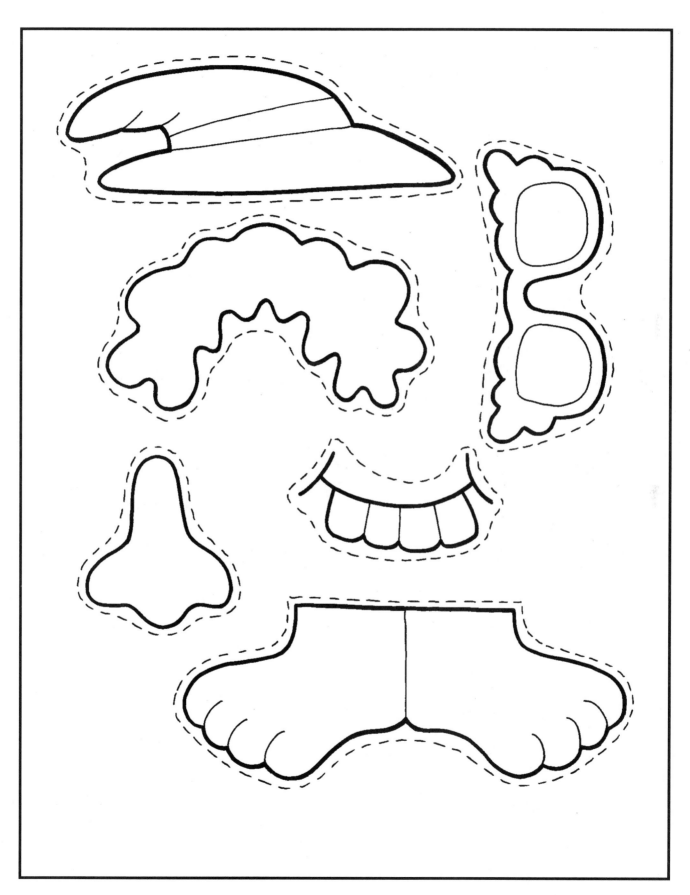

Ff Patterns

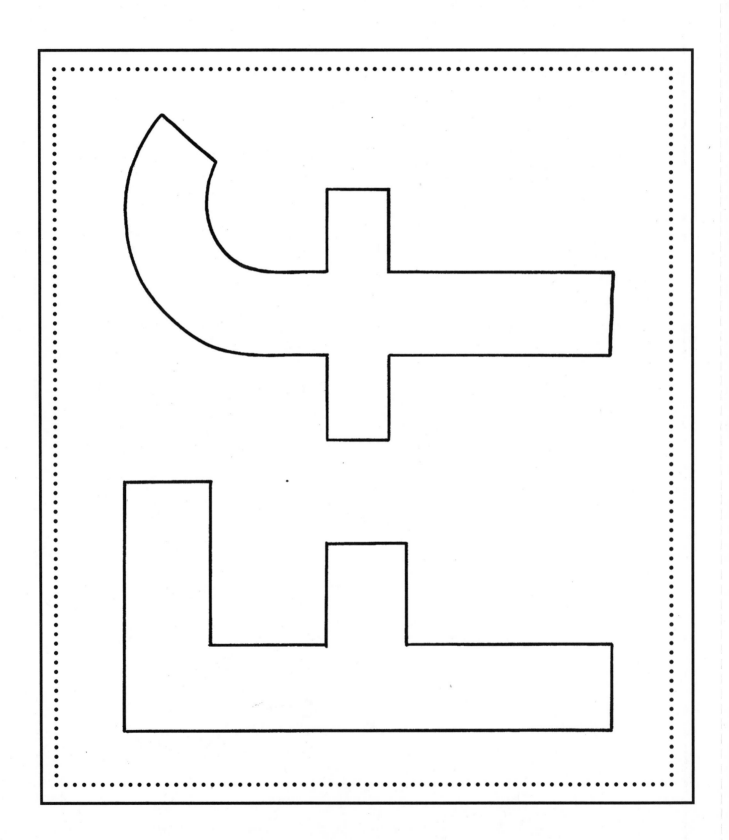

WEB HUNTERS

Materials:
Spider patterns (p. 62), yarn or thread, scissors, crayons or markers, two-sided tape

Preparation:
Duplicate and cut out the Spider patterns. Make enough spiders for each child to have one. Wrap yarn or thread around objects (such as the legs of a chair), and fasten with two-sided tape to create webs.

Spider Facts:
- Spiders live all over the world: in swamps, in jungles, in the Arctic, in fields, in houses, by the ocean, and so on.
- Spiders can spin different kinds of silk: fuzzy, smooth, thick, thin, dry, and sticky.
- Some spiders are web builders. They catch their prey in webs.
- Wandering spiders move from place to place in search of food.

Directions:
1. Explain that spiders spin webs from silk that they create. Webs are made to catch insects. Spiders then eat the insects.
2. Tell the class that they will become web hunters and will hunt for webs in the classroom.
3. Once the children locate the webs, give each child a cut-out spider to color with crayons and tape to the webs.

Literature Link:
- *Tarantulas: The Biggest Spiders* by Alexander L. Crosby (Walker, 1981).
This resource is filled with facts and photographs of tarantulas.

Spider Patterns

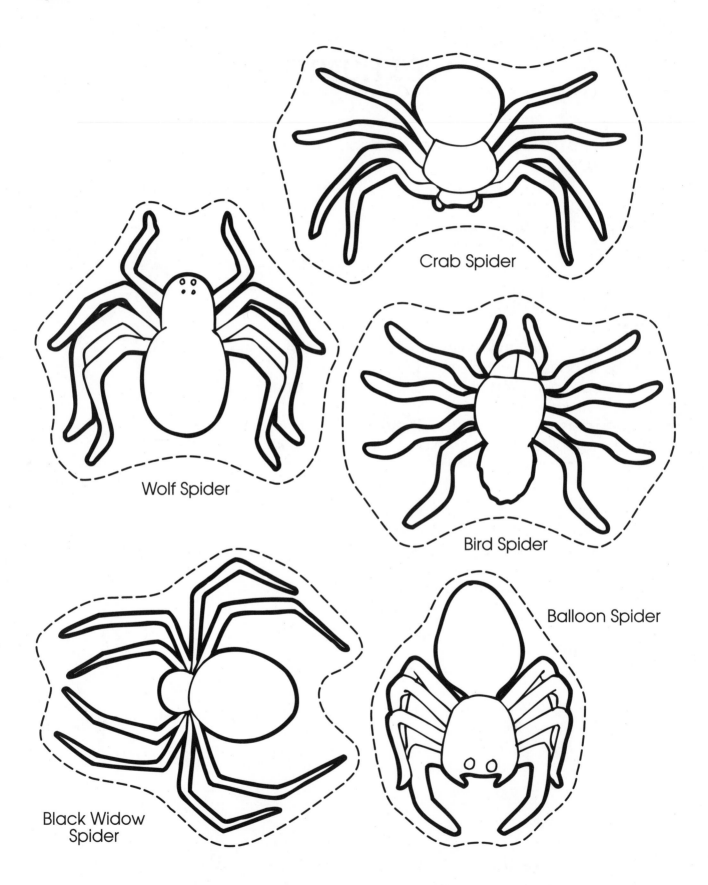

Crab Spider

Wolf Spider

Bird Spider

Balloon Spider

Black Widow Spider

THE BAT ECHO

Materials:
Flashlight

Preparation:
None

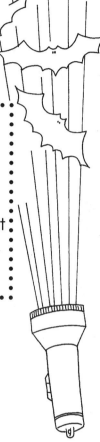

Bat Facts:
- Bats fly in the dark without bumping into anything.
- Bats can find and catch insects that fly in the dark.
- Bats send out high-pitched noises that echo back to them, letting them know what objects are in their paths. Echoes tell bats what kinds of insects are flying in front of them and how fast the insects are going!
- Finding their way by listening to echoes of their own sounds is called "echolocation."

Directions:
1. Dim the lights in the room.
2. Ask for a volunteer to be a bat. Have this child make a high-pitched sound.
3. Wave the flashlight from the child to an object across the room. Rotate the light as it travels. Explain that the light represents sound waves from the bat's screech. Rest the light on the object.
4. Explain that when sound waves hit an object, they bounce back as an echo. Rotate the light back to the bat.
5. Tell the children that a bat hears the echo and knows where the object is. (The child pretending to be the bat can now walk to the object and touch it.) A bat can do this in total darkness!
6. Ask for other volunteers to be bats and to rotate the flashlight.

Literature Link:
- *The World of Bats* by Virginia Harrison, adapted from Helen Riley's "The Bat in the Cave," photographs by Oxford Scientific Films (Gareth Stevens, 1989).
This book includes facts as well as four-color photographs of bats.

JACK-O'-LANTERN COUNTING

· ·

Materials:
Jack-o'-lantern patterns (p. 65), Jack-o'-lantern Math Rhyme
(pp. 66-67), crayons, scissors, envelopes (one per child)

Preparation:
Duplicate a copy of the Jack-o'-lantern patterns and the
Jack-o'-lantern Math Rhyme for each child. Make one copy
of the Jack-o'-lantern Math Rhyme to read to the students.

Directions:
1. Give each child a copy of the Jack-o'-lantern patterns to color
and cut out.
2. Read the Jack-o'-lantern Math Rhyme to the children.
3. Have the children manipulate the patterns while the rhyme is
read aloud.
4. Children can store the patterns and rhymes in envelopes for
at-home practice.

Literature Link:
• *It's Pumpkin Time* by Zoe Hall, illustrated by Shari Halpern (The Blue
Sky Press, 1994).
A brother and sister prepare for Halloween by growing a jack-o'-
lantern patch. At the end of the book is an explanation of how
pumpkin seeds grow underground.

Two little jack-o'-lanterns sit beneath a tree.
Another one joins them, and then there are... THREE.

Jack-o'-lantern Patterns

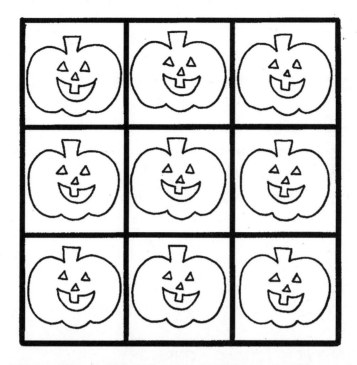

65

Jack-o'-lantern Math Rhyme (1-5)

One little jack-o'-lantern
Was feeling sort of blue.
Another one cheered him up,
And then there were . . . (two).

Two little jack-o'-lanterns
Sat beneath a tree.
Another one joined them,
And then there were . . . (three).

Three little jack-o'-lanterns
Sat upon the floor.
Another one stopped in for fun,
And then there were . . . (four).

Four little jack-o'-lanterns
Went out for a drive.
They picked up another one,
And then there were . . . (five).

Jack-o'-lantern Math Rhymes (5-10)

Five little jack-o'-lanterns
Were out doing kicks.
Another one stopped by to dance,
And then there were . . . (six).

Six little jack-o'-lanterns
Looked up at the heavens.
Another stopped to stargaze,
And then there were . . . (seven).

Seven little jack-o'-lanterns
Went out for a date.
A friend joined up with them
To make their party . . . (eight).

Eight little jack-o'-lanterns
Were feeling pretty fine.
They stopped by a friend's house,
And then there were . . . (nine).

Nine little jack-o'-lanterns
Went back home again.
Their mother was waiting up,
And with her that made . . . (ten).

THE BAT CAVE

. . . .

Materials:
Bat Counting patterns (p. 70), Bat Math Rhyme (pp. 71-74), scissors, black crayons, envelopes (one per child)

Preparation:
Duplicate a copy of the Bat Counting patterns and the Bat Math Rhyme for each child. Duplicate one copy of the Bat Math Rhyme to read aloud.

Bat Facts:
- Bats sleep upside down.
- Bats are known for sleeping in caves.

Directions:
1. Have the children color and cut out the Bat Counting patterns.
2. Read the Bat Math Rhyme to the children.
3. Have the children manipulate the patterns while the rhyme is read aloud.
4. Children can store the patterns and rhymes in envelopes for additional at-home practice.

Option:
Secure a clothesline across the classroom. Duplicate copies of the Large Bat pattern (p. 69) for each child to color and cut out. Use clothespins to clip each bat onto the clothesline. When all bats are hanging, use them for counting exercises, adding, and subtracting.

Literature Link:
- *Stellaluna* by Janell Cannon (Harcourt Brace, 1993).
Stellaluna, a baby bat, is raised by a bird family. Available on audiotape from High Windy Audio at (800) 637-8679.

Large Bat Pattern

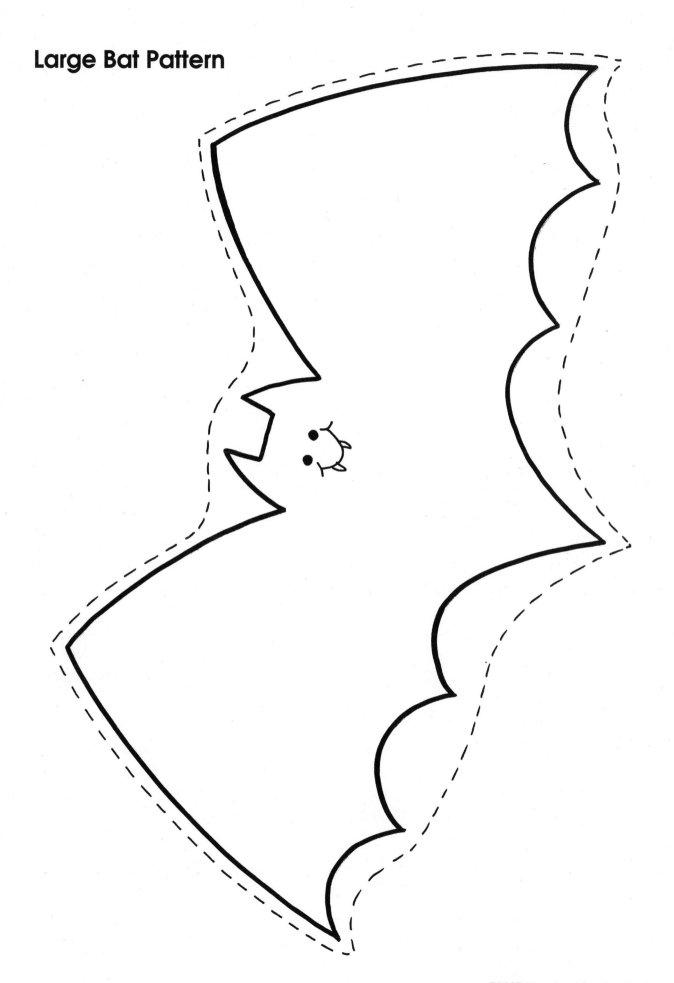

Bat Counting Patterns

Bat Math Rhyme (10-5)

Ten little bats were trying to behave.
They hung upside down from their feet in a cave.
One little bat thought it was time to dine.
He flew out of the cave all alone, leaving . . . (nine).

Nine little bats were trying to behave.
They hung upside down from their feet in a cave.
One little bat said it was time she ate.
She flew out of the cave all alone, leaving . . . (eight).

Eight little bats were trying to behave.
They hung upside down from their feet in a cave.
One little bat took a look out at the heavens.
He flew out of the cave all alone, leaving . . . (seven).

Seven little bats were trying to behave.
They hung upside down from their feet in a cave.
One little bat showed off her flying tricks.
She flew out of the cave all alone, leaving . . . (six).

Six little bats were trying to behave.
They hung upside down from their feet in a cave.
One little bat said he could do a dive.
He flew out of the cave all alone, leaving . . . (five).

71

Bat Math Rhyme (5-1)

Five little bats were trying to behave.
They hung upside down from their feet in a cave.
One hungry bat said that she wanted some more.
She saw a bug outside, and flew off, leaving . . . (four).

Four little bats were trying to behave.
They hung upside down from their feet in a cave.
One little bat said, "Hey, pals, look at me!"
He did some fancy flying in the sky, leaving . . . (three).

Three little bats were trying to behave.
They hung upside down from their feet in a cave.
One little bat said she had something to do.
She flapped her tiny wings, and flew off, leaving . . . (two).

Two little bats were trying to behave.
They hung upside down from their feet in a cave.
One little bat said he wanted to have fun.
He said, "I'll see you later," and took off, leaving . . . (one).

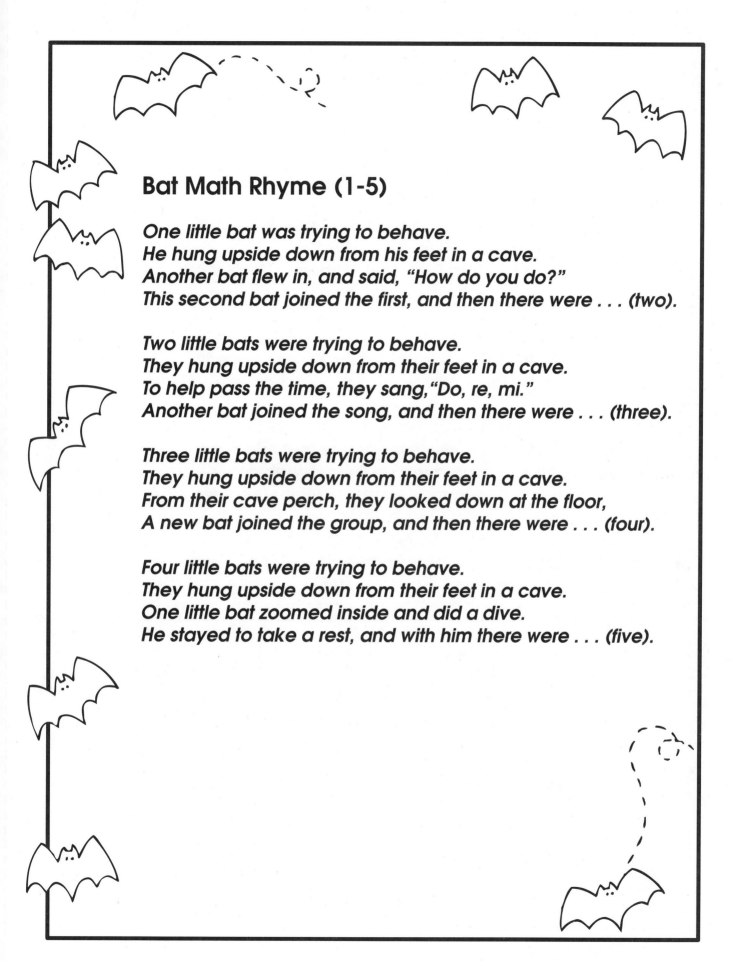

Bat Math Rhyme (1-5)

One little bat was trying to behave.
He hung upside down from his feet in a cave.
Another bat flew in, and said, "How do you do?"
This second bat joined the first, and then there were . . . (two).

Two little bats were trying to behave.
They hung upside down from their feet in a cave.
To help pass the time, they sang,"Do, re, mi."
Another bat joined the song, and then there were . . . (three).

Three little bats were trying to behave.
They hung upside down from their feet in a cave.
From their cave perch, they looked down at the floor,
A new bat joined the group, and then there were . . . (four).

Four little bats were trying to behave.
They hung upside down from their feet in a cave.
One little bat zoomed inside and did a dive.
He stayed to take a rest, and with him there were . . . (five).

73

Bat Math Rhyme (5-10)

Five little bats were trying to behave.
They hung upside down from their feet in a cave.
These five bats showed off their flying tricks.
Another one joined the show, and then there were . . . (six).

Six little bats were trying to behave.
They hung upside down from their feet in a cave.
These six bats flew upwards toward the heavens,
Another bat joined them, and then there were . . . (seven).

Seven little bats were trying to behave.
They hung upside down from their feet in a cave.
All the little bats cleaned up before their dates,
Another bat joined the group, and then there were . . . (eight).

Eight little bats were trying to behave.
They hung upside down from their feet in a cave.
All the little bats got ready to dine,
Another bat joined the group, and then there were . . . (nine).

Nine little bats were trying to behave.
They hung upside down from their feet in a cave.
All the little bats went out to fly again,
Another bat flew with them, and then there were . . . (ten).

Ten little bats were trying to behave.
They hung upside down from their feet in a cave.
The sun was big and bright.
The bats closed their eyes tight.
They wrapped their wings around themselves,
And waited for the night.

CHALK MONSTERS

Materials:

Monster Award patterns (p. 76), black construction paper, colored chalk, scissors, tape

Preparation:

Duplicate the Monster Awards, color, and cut out.

Directions:

1. Provide black construction paper and colored chalk for children to use to make chalk monsters. Encourage the children to use their imaginations. *Note*: Remind the children to avoid placing their arms on their papers while they are drawing. The chalk can smear!
2. Tape the completed pictures on a "Cheerful Chalk Monsters" bulletin board.
3. Give each picture a Monster Award. Label each award. For example, make an award for the scariest monster, hungriest monster, silliest monster, funniest monster, and so on.

Option:

Spray the finished pictures with hair spray, a great chalk fixative. *Note*: Do this away from the children.

Literature Link:

• *Monsters* by Russell Hoban, illustrated by Quentin Blake (Scholastic, 1989).
John is a little boy who likes to draw monsters. His love of monsters increases until his parents take him to a psychiatrist. The doctor comes to a monstrous end!

Monster Award Patterns

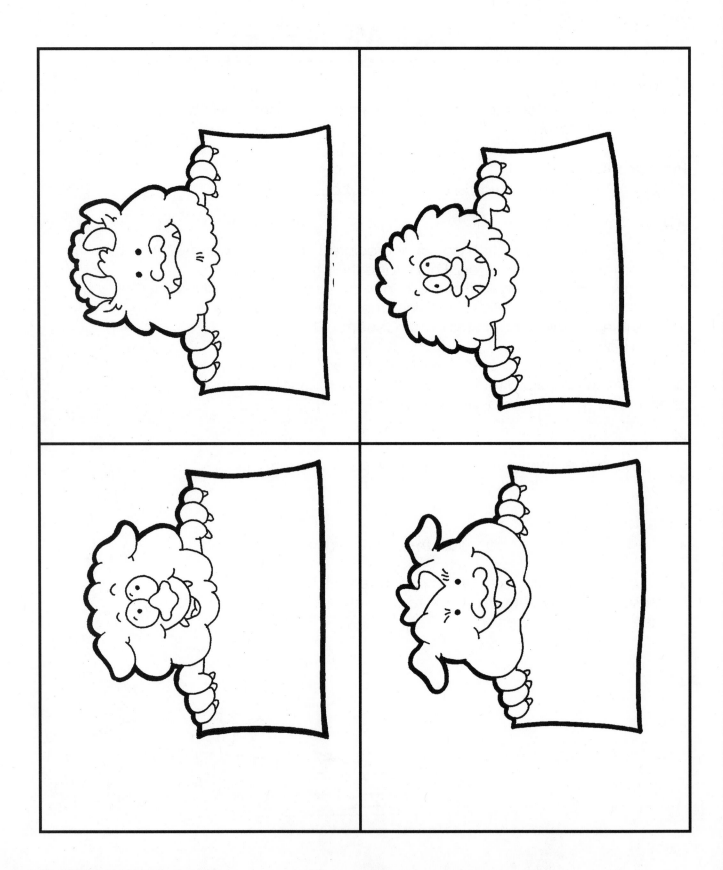

EGG SAC BAGS

∙ ∙

Materials:
Small paper bags (one per child), white paint in pie tins, paint-brushes, scissors, newspaper, yarn

Preparation:
Cut a piece of yarn approximately one arm-length long for each child.

Directions:
1. Explain to the children that mother spiders wrap their eggs in egg sacs. The children are going to make sacs from craft materials.
2. Have the children tear strips of newspaper to use to stuff their paper bags. These bags will represent the egg sacs.
3. When the egg sacs are plump with newspaper, help the children tie the bags closed with yarn.
4. Provide paint and brushes for children to use to paint their egg sacs white.
5. When the egg sacs have dried, hang them around the classroom by the yarn ties.

Literature Link:
• *The Very Busy Spider* by Eric Carle (Philomel, 1984).
This book will hold special appeal, as the spider and web are raised off the page.

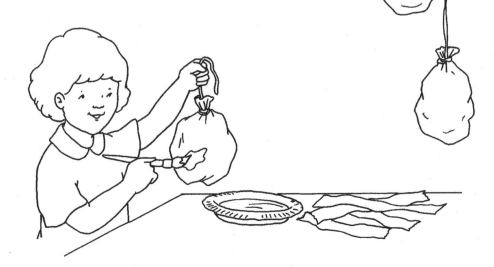

BUG ME!

Materials:
Insect pattern (p. 79), tape

Preparation:
Duplicate and enlarge the Insect pattern.

Insect Facts:
- Insects have six legs.
- Insects have two feelers or antennae.
- Insects have two or more wings.
- Insects have three body segments.
- Insects have two or four eyes.
- Insects live everywhere. There are more insects in the world than people!

Directions:
1. Have the children sit together in a circle. Post the Insect pattern where all the children can see it.
2. Ask for a volunteer. Tell the children that together you are going to find out if this child is a human or an insect. (Expect laughter!)
3. Use the facts to observe whether the child has the different insect characteristics.
4. Once you have established that you have a child (and not an insect), have children observe the Insect pattern further.

Option:
Take the children on a five-minute walk outside. They should see at least one insect. Discuss the different insects sighted once you're back in the room.

Literature Link:
- *Bugs for Dinner?* by Sam and Beryl Epstein, illustrated by Walter Gaffney-Kessell (Macmillan, 1989).
This informative book explores the eating habits of animals and insects.

Insect Pattern

LET'S WING IT

. . . .

Materials:
Winged Insects patterns (p. 81), crayons, scissors, colored construction paper, glue

Preparation:
Duplicate a copy of the Winged Insects patterns for each child.

Wing Facts:
- Most birds have feathered wings.
- Ladybugs' wings are hidden under hard protective shells.
- Butterflies' wings are soft and powdery.

Directions:
1. Have the children sit together in a circle and brainstorm different creatures that have wings, for example, birds, beetles, butterflies, ladybugs, and bats.
2. Discuss why wings might be helpful. Wings allow creatures to move fast, to travel over water, to escape from enemies, and to look for food.
3. Give each child a copy of the Winged Insects patterns. Have the children circle the pictures of the insects that have wings.
4. Explain that insects come in many different colors. The children can color their insects, cut them out, and glue them to construction paper.

Literature Link:
- *The Honeybee and the Robber* by Eric Carle (Philomel, 1981). One bee saves the hive when a bear attacks it.

Winged Insects Patterns

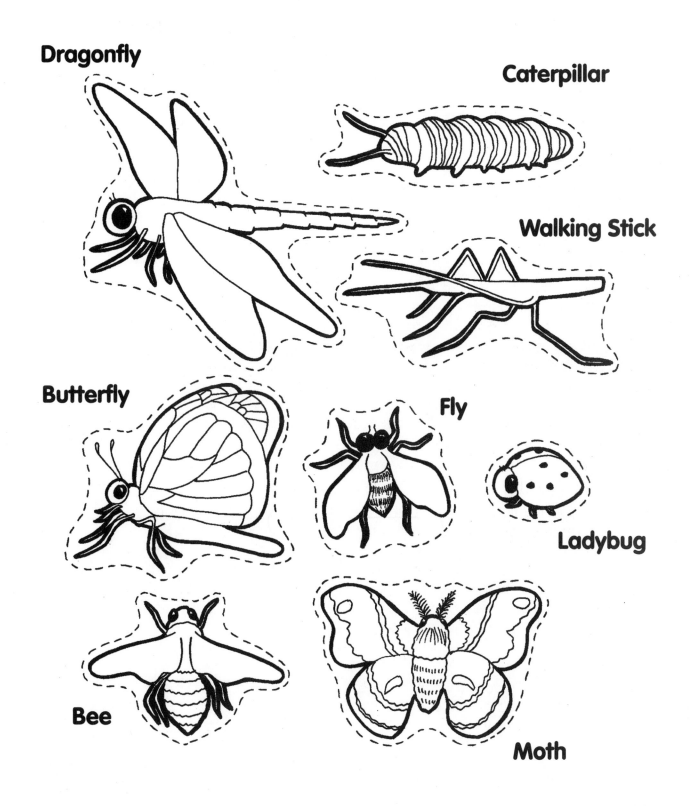

Dragonfly

Caterpillar

Walking Stick

Butterfly

Fly

Ladybug

Bee

Moth

**Things with Wings
Science**

THE POLLINATION STATION

Materials:
Two sheets of blue construction paper, marker, one sheet of white paper, cornmeal, scissors, glue, crayons

Preparation:
Use the marker to draw simple flowers on both sheets of blue paper. Place these papers close together on a table. Sprinkle cornmeal on the first sheet of paper only. Label the table with a sign that says "Pollination Station."

Pollination Facts:
- New flowers grow from seeds.
- Flowers need two parts to make a seed: egg cells and pollen.
- Some insects help flowers grow by pollinating the flowers. This means that they transfer pollen from one flower to another.
- When a butterfly lands on a flower to feed, some of the flower's pollen sticks to it. The pollen comes off the butterfly's legs when it lands on the next flower. This helps the flower make seeds.

Directions:
1. Have the children take turns at the Pollination Station. The children can pretend their fingertips are butterflies' feet and use two fingers to "walk" on the first sheet of paper. The children's fingers will pick up the cornmeal "pollen."
2. Have the children use their fingers to move to the next sheet of paper and "walk" their fingers around, spreading the "pollen."
3. The children can observe the two sheets of paper when everyone has had a turn at the Pollination Station.

Literature Link:
- *From Flower to Flower: Animals and Pollination* by Patricia Lauber, photographs by Jerome Wexler (Crown, 1986).
This resource has many pictures of insects pollinating flowers.

FEATHER SCIENTISTS

Materials:
A variety of feathers (available at art stores and teacher supply stores), a scale and balancing items, a tub of water (or a water table)

Preparation:
Place a variety of feathers on a table or rug area. Fill a tub with water, or set up a water table.

Directions:
1. Explain that the children are going to be "feather scientists."
2. Have the children observe the weight of the feathers, the feel of the feathers, and the look of the feathers.
3. Explain that birds have special glands that spread oil on their feathers to make them waterproof. Have children observe what happens when they drop a feather in a tub of water.

Extension:
Duplicate the Bird and Feather patterns (p. 84) for children to color and cut out. Post the cutouts on a bulletin board with pieces of yarn matching the birds to their feathers.

Literature Link:
• *Feathers* by Dorothy Hinshaw-Patent (Dutton, 1992).
This resource describes, in text and photographs, birds' feathers.

Bird and Feather Patterns

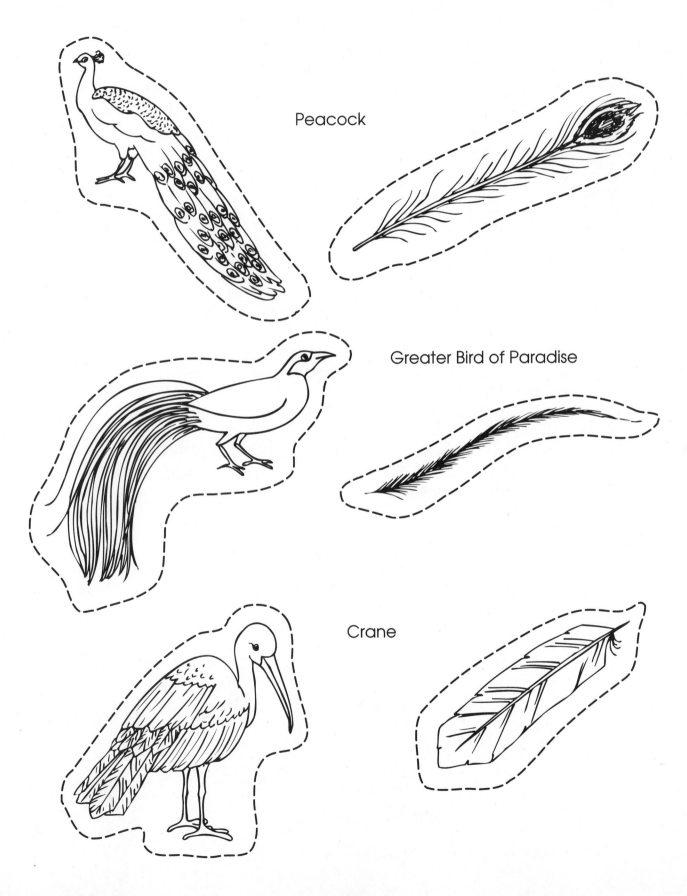

Peacock

Greater Bird of Paradise

Crane

SPOT FINDERS

Materials:
Ladybug pattern (p. 86), Ladybug Math Rhyme (pp. 87-88), crayons (red and black), scissors, glue

Preparation:
Duplicate one copy of the Ladybug pattern for each child. Duplicate one copy of the Ladybug Math Rhyme to read to the students.

Directions:
1. Give each child a Ladybug pattern to color and cut out. Help children cut out the dots if needed. (As an option, use black dots hole-punched from black construction paper.)
2. Have the children place the ladybugs and spots on their desks.
3. As you read the math rhyme, have the children move the spots onto the ladybugs.
4. Children can glue spots to their ladybugs after the lesson.
5. Post the completed pictures on a "Lucky Ladybug" bulletin board.

Literature Link:
• *Lady Bugatti* by Joyce Maxner, illustrated by Kevin Hawkes (Lothrop, 1991).
When Lady Bugatti throws a dinner party, all of her insect friends want to come! This new classic is told in rhyme.

Ladybug Pattern

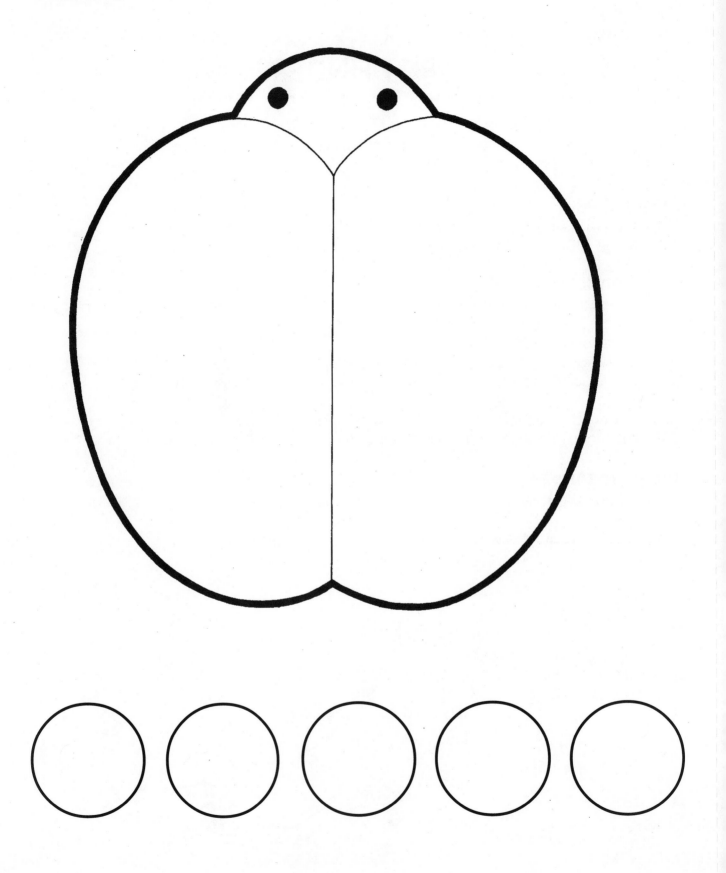

Ladybug Math Rhyme (0-5)

This math rhyme can be sung to the tune of "This Old Man."

Ladybug has no spots,
Her red shell has no black dots.
So she goes out shopping
And buys herself a dot.
Now her shell has . . . (one) black spot.

Ladybug has one spot,
But she wants another dot.
So she goes out shopping
And buys another dot.
Now her shell has . . . (two) black spots!

Ladybug has two spots,
But she wants another dot.
So she goes out shopping
And buys another dot.
Now her shell has . . . (three) black spots!

Ladybug has three spots,
But she wants another dot.
So she goes out shopping
And buys another dot.
Now her shell has . . . (four) black spots!

Ladybug has four spots,
But she wants another dot.
So she goes out shopping
And buys another dot.
Now her shell has . . . (five) black spots!

Ladybug Math Rhyme (5-0)

This math rhyme can be sung to the tune of "This Old Man."

Ladybug has five spots,
But she's tired of her dots.
So she takes one off her shell,
And gets rid of a dot.
Now her shell has . . . (four) black spots!

Ladybug has four spots,
But she's tired of her dots.
So she takes one off her shell,
And gets rid of a dot.
Now her shell has . . . (three) black spots!

Ladybug has three spots,
But she's tired of her dots.
So she takes one off her shell,
And gets rid of a dot.
Now her shell has . . . (two) black spots!

Ladybug has two spots,
But she's tired of her dots.
So she takes one off her shell,
And gets rid of a dot.
Now her shell has . . . (one) black spot!

Ladybug has one spot,
But she's tired of her dot.
So she takes it off her shell,
And gets rid of the dot.
Now her shell has . . . (no) black spots!

Ladybug Number Sets

🐞	1	🐞🐞	2
🐞🐞🐞	3	🐞🐞🐞🐞	4
🐞🐞🐞🐞🐞	5	🐞🐞🐞🐞🐞🐞	6
🐞🐞🐞🐞🐞🐞🐞	7	🐞🐞🐞🐞🐞🐞🐞🐞	8
🐞🐞🐞🐞🐞🐞🐞🐞🐞	9	🐞🐞🐞🐞🐞🐞🐞🐞🐞🐞	10

CAN YOU SEE ME?

Materials:
Bird pattern (p. 91), crayons, construction paper in a variety of colors matching the colors of the crayons, glue or paste, scissors

Preparation:
Duplicate a copy of the Bird pattern for each child.

Directions:
1. Review the definition of the word "camouflage" with the children. Explain that birds are often able to hide from danger because of their coloring. For example, white birds blend with snowy backgrounds and multicolored birds blend easily in jungles.
2. Give each child a copy of the Bird pattern to cut out.
3. Have each child choose one crayon to use to color the Bird pattern.
4. Once children have finished coloring, each child can choose a sheet of construction paper that would best camouflage his or her bird. Encourage the children to experiment with many colors to find the right ones.
5. Provide glue or paste for children to use to attach their birds to their chosen sheets of construction paper.
6. Post the completed pictures on a "Creative Camouflage" bulletin board.

Literature Link:
• *Animal Camouflage: A Closer Look* by Joyce Powzyk (Bradbury, 1990).
This book shows both insects and other animals camouflaged in nature.

Bird Pattern

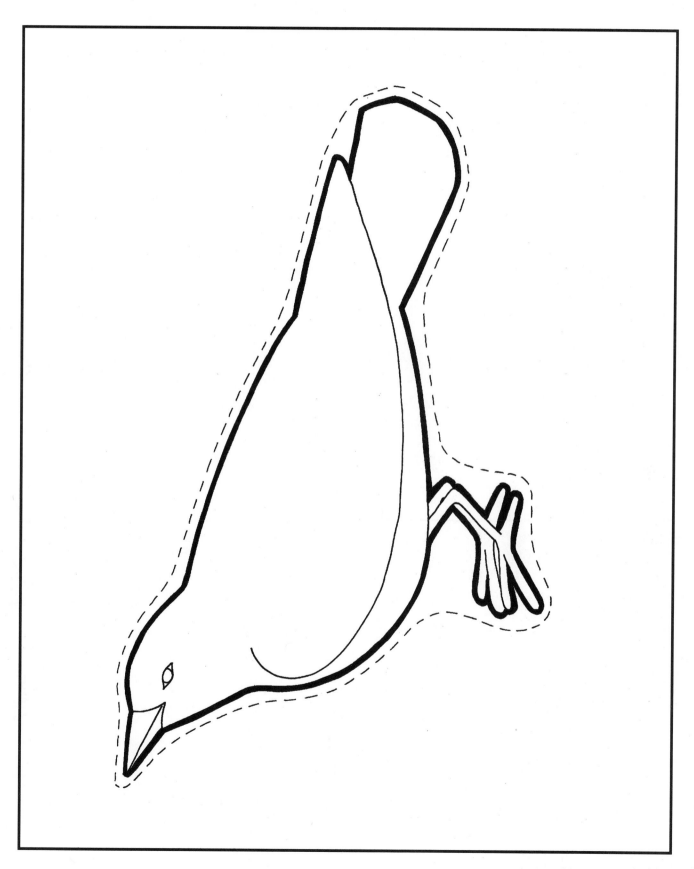

EYEDROPPER BUTTERFLIES

Materials:
White tissue paper, eyedroppers (available cheaply in bulk), food coloring, small bowls, newsprint, yarn, green construction paper, felt pen, pipe cleaners, transparent tape, glue, scissors

Preparation:
Cover a long table with newsprint. On this table, place eyedroppers near bowls of food coloring. (The food coloring may be thinned with water.) On a separate table, arrange green construction paper, scissors, tape, glue, and pipe cleaners.

Directions:
1. Give each child a sheet of tissue paper to decorate at the "coloring stations." Have children drop food coloring onto their tissue paper, which will be the butterfly wings. Suggest that the children put only two or three drops of food coloring on top of each other—the colors won't become as muddy this way.
2. While the wings are drying, children can go to the next table and cut out thin butterfly bodies from the green construction paper.
3. Children can glue or tape pipe cleaners to the butterfly bodies.
4. Help children print their names on their butterfly bodies.
5. When the wings have dried, demonstrate how to pinch the top and bottom edges of the wings together in the middle and fasten with transparent tape.
6. Children can tape the butterfly bodies to the wings.
7. Post the swarm of butterflies on a wall or bulletin board.

Literature Link:
• *The Butterfly Hunt* by Yoshi (Picture Book Studio, 1990). This book is beautifully illustrated, with pictures of many different types of butterflies on the front and back covers.

Things with Wings
Games

BUTTERFLY CONCENTRATION

Materials:
Butterfly patterns (p. 94), crayons, scissors, clear Contac paper (optional)

Preparation:
For each set, make two copies of the Butterfly patterns. Color the two copies exactly alike and cut the cards out. Laminate or cover with clear Contac paper, if desired. (This will protect the cards and make them last longer.) Teach children how to play the game of Concentration.

Directions to Play:
1. All of the cards are spread out face down.
2. The first child turns two cards over.
3. If the cards match, the child keeps the pair and goes again.
4. If the cards don't match, the child turns the cards face down, and the next child takes a turn.
5. Play continues until all of the cards have been matched.

Literature Link:
• *Monarch Butterfly* by Gail Gibbons (Holiday House, 1989). This book explains in simple text the stages of life of a monarch butterfly.

Butterfly Patterns

Chapter Three
Thanksgiving and Senses

THANKSGIVING MEALS

. . . .

Materials:
Thanksgiving Food patterns (p. 97), crayons, scissors, glue, paper plates (one per student)

Preparation:
Duplicate one copy of the Thanksgiving Food patterns for each child.

Directions:
1. Have the students discuss Thanksgiving meals they have eaten.
2. Give each child a Thanksgiving Food pattern to color and cut out. Explain that corn was served at the original Thanksgiving feast.
3. Have children arrange and glue the food cutouts on the plates.
4. Post the completed meals on a "Yummy Thanksgiving!" bulletin board, or send them home with the children.

Extension:
Host a food drive at your school for families in need. Students can design and color flyers to post throughout the school. The food cutouts from the Thanksgiving Food patterns can be used on the flyers.

Literature Link:
• *Albert's Thanksgiving* by Leslie Tryon (Atheneum, 1994).
It is Thanksgiving in Pleasant Valley, and Albert the duck has his hands full preparing for the PTA-sponsored Thanksgiving feast!

Thanksgiving Food Patterns

THANKSGIVING GOLD

. . . .

Materials:
Turkey pattern (p. 99), Egg patterns (p. 100), scissors, gold crayons, glue, felt board, felt, gold glitter (optional), colored construction paper

Preparation:
Duplicate a copy of the Turkey pattern and Egg patterns for each child. Decorate one set using a gold crayon and gold glitter. Glue a piece of felt on the back of each pattern.

Directions:
1. Tell students the story of the goose that laid the golden eggs. (Or read it from one of the Literature Links listed below.)
2. Explain to the students that you have a turkey that lays golden eggs. Put the turkey on the felt board.
3. Tell the students that in each of this turkey's eggs is a word starting with the letter "g." As you bring out each felt egg, read the word on the egg. Have the students repeat the words with you.
4. When you have finished placing the eggs, let students take turns posting the eggs and saying the words.
5. Give each child a paper copy of the turkey and eggs to color, cut out, and glue to construction paper sheets.
6. Post the completed turkeys and eggs on a "Good as Gold" bulletin board.

Literature Links:
• *Aesop's Fables: A Classic Illustrated Edition*, compiled by Russell Ash and Bernard Higton (Chronicle, 1990).
• *Baby's Own Aesop* by Walter Crane (Warne, no date).
• *Jack Kent's Fables of Aesop* by Jack Kent (Parents', 1972).

Turkey Pattern

Egg Patterns

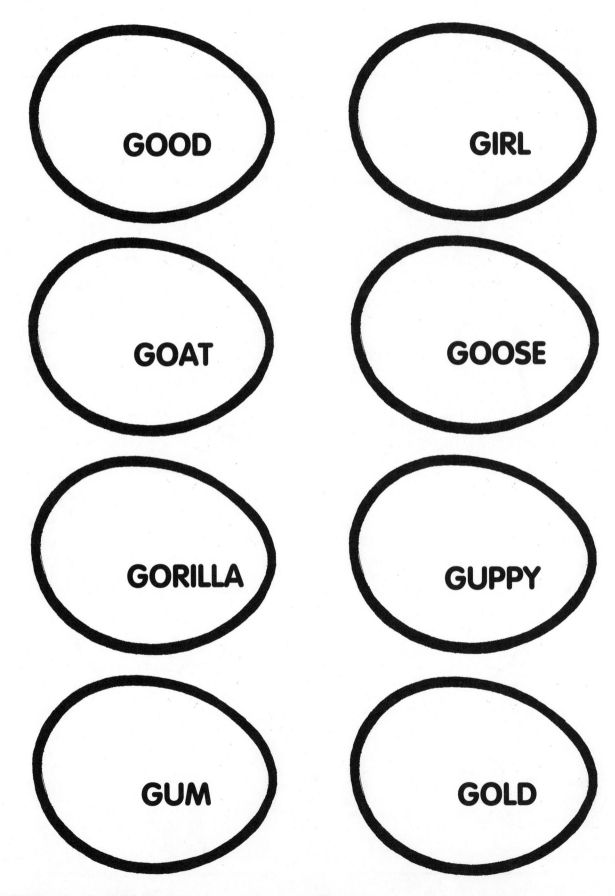

GOOD

GIRL

GOAT

GOOSE

GORILLA

GUPPY

GUM

GOLD

Gg Patterns

THANKSGIVING HATS

. . . .

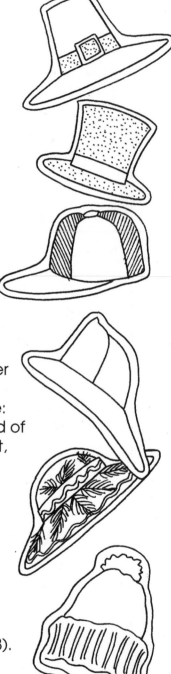

Materials:
Hat patterns (p. 103), crayons, scissors, glue, art supplies (including sequins, fabric scraps, lace, yarn, feathers, and rickrack)

Preparation:
Duplicate a copy of the Hat patterns for each child.

Directions:
1. Have the children say the word "hat" and listen to the "h" sound.
2. Teach the children the Hat Rhyme. Say it slowly at first, and let the children repeat it with you.

> **Hat Rhyme**
> **A hat is something I wear on my head.**
> **I have a green hat and one that is red.**
> **I have a farmer's hat and a Pilgrim's hat, too.**
> **I like to wear hats . . . do you?**

3. Point to a child when you finish the rhyme and let that child answer the question. Once children learn the rhyme, they can play this with each other, posing the question to a different child each time. (Note: You can change the types of hats in the rhyme. For example, instead of "farmer's hat" you might say, "I have a summer hat and a winter hat, too.")
4. Give each child a copy of the Hat patterns to color, cut out, and decorate using feathers, sequins, and other art supplies.
5. Post the completed hats on a "Hooray for Hats!" bulletin board.

Extension:
Have children bring in their favorite hat from home for show and tell.

Literature Link:
• *The 500 Hats of Bartholomew Cubbins* by Dr. Seuss (Vanguard, 1938). Each time Bartholomew tries to take his hat off for the king, there's another hat on his head!

Hat Patterns

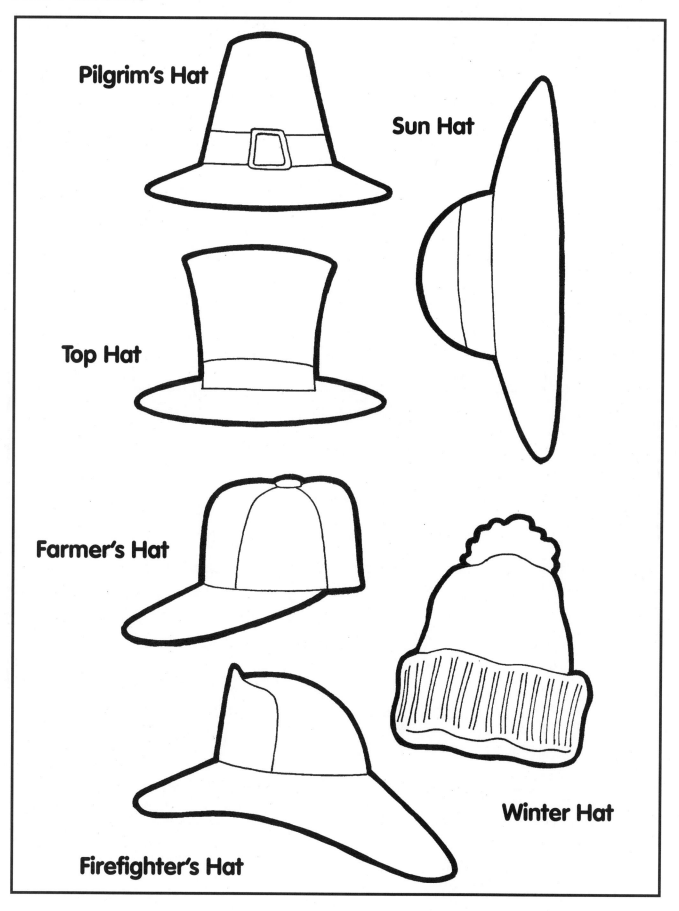

Pilgrim's Hat

Sun Hat

Top Hat

Farmer's Hat

Winter Hat

Firefighter's Hat

I LIKE IT!

. . . .

Materials:
"I Like It" pattern (p. 106), "Ii" patterns (p. 107), black felt pen, crayons

Preparation:
Duplicate a copy of the "I Like It" pattern for each child.

Directions:
1. Explain that the letter "I" is also the word "I."
2. Hold up the "Ii" patterns as you have the children say "I."
3. Teach the children the "I Like It" chant. Clap to establish a rhythm. At the end of the chant, ask a volunteer to think of a food he or she likes to eat.
4. Repeat the chant and substitute the new word for "turkey." (You can substitute other Thanksgiving food words: stuffing, cranberries, corn, gravy, biscuits, squash, sweet potatoes, pumpkin pie.)

> **I Like It!**
> *I like it!*
> *I love it!*
> *I want more of it!*
> *I chewed it!*
> *I ate it!*
> *I like turkey!*

5. Give each child a copy of the "I Like It" pattern.
6. Children can use crayons to draw foods they like on the pattern.

Option:
Provide old magazines from which children can cut out foods or other items that they like. Children can use glue to make an "I Like It" collage.

Literature Link:
• *Green Eggs and Ham* by Dr. Seuss (Random House, 1960).
No matter how much Sam pushes, the narrator of this classic story won't try green eggs and ham . . . at least not until the end.

I Like It! Pattern

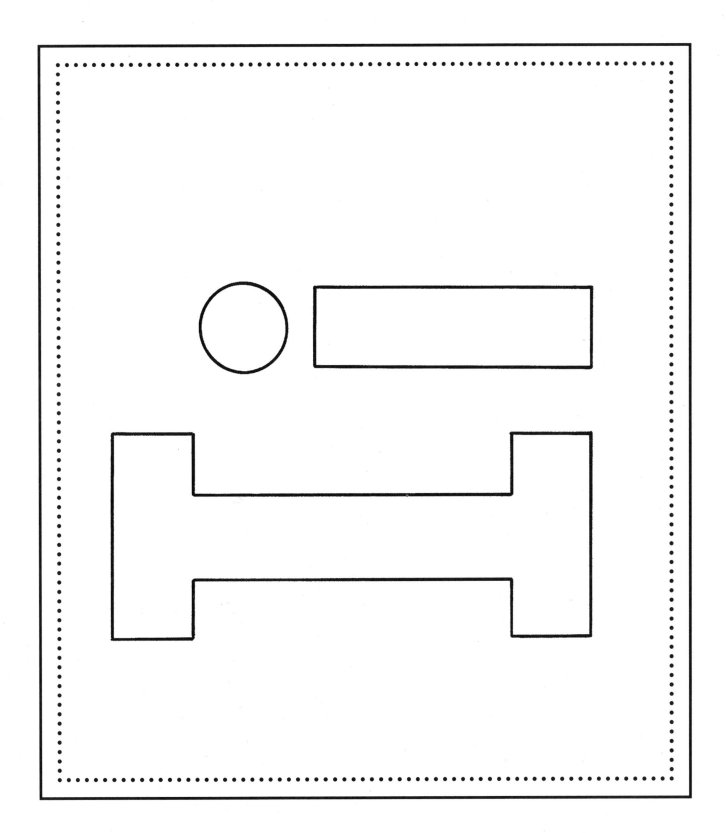

THANKSGIVING HARVEST

· ·

Materials:
Parsley seeds, dirt, plastic cups (one per child), water, masking tape, felt pen

Preparation:
Fill each plastic cup with a small amount of dirt (deep enough to bury a few parsley seeds)

Directions:
1. Explain that the original Thanksgiving was a celebration of the Pilgrims' first harvest.
2. Give each child a few parsley seeds and a plastic cup partially filled with dirt.
3. Have children plant their parsley seeds in their plastic cups.
4. Help children add a small amount of water to the planters.
5. Label the planters with the children's names using masking tape and a felt pen.
6. Place the planters in a sunny spot.
7. Have children observe their seeds every day. Help them to determine when water is needed. (*Note*: Do not overwater!)
8. The parsley seeds should grow fairly quickly. When the parsley has grown, help children "harvest" it.

Option:
Serve the washed parsley with cream cheese and crackers at snack time.

Literature Link:
• *Vegetable Garden* by Douglas Florian (Harcourt, 1991). This rhyming book tells of a family that plants and harvests a vegetable garden.

TEN LITTLE TURKEYS

Materials:
Turkey patterns (p. 110), Turkey Math Problems (pp. 111-112), crayons, scissors, envelopes (one per child)

Preparation:
Duplicate a copy of the Turkey patterns and the Turkey Math Problems for each child.

Directions:
1. Give each child an envelope and a copy of the Turkey patterns to color and cut out.
2. Read the Turkey Math Problems to the children. As you recite the math problems, have the children move the turkeys, one by one, into the envelope. The children can count the turkeys to help them answer the math problems.
3. Children can store the patterns and rhymes in envelopes for additional at-home practice.

Literature Link:
• *'Twas the Night Before Thanksgiving* by Dav Pilkey (Orchard, 1990). A group of children on a field trip to a farm rescue eight turkeys in this silly retelling of the famous Christmas rhyme.

Turkey Patterns

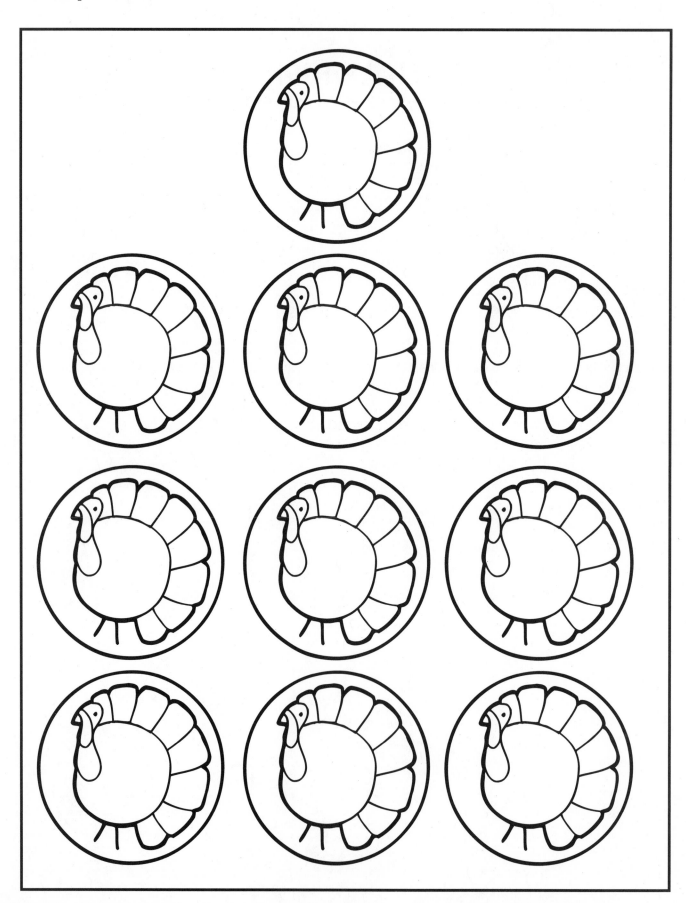

Turkey Math Problems (10-5)

Ten little turkeys sat in their pen.
"Hide, turkeys, hide!" said the little red hen.
One little turkey flew far away,
But the other . . . (nine) decided to stay.

Nine little turkeys sat in their pen.
"Hide, turkeys, hide!" said the little red hen.
One little turkey flew out of the gate,
And when he was gone, there were . . . (eight).

Eight little turkeys sat in their pen.
"Hide, turkeys, hide!" said the little red hen.
One little turkey flew far away,
But the other . . . (seven) decided to stay.

Seven little turkeys sat in their pen.
"Hide, turkeys, hide!" said the little red hen.
One little turkey hid with the chicks,
And when she was gone, there were . . . (six).

Six little turkeys sat in their pen.
"Hide, turkeys, hide!" said the little red hen.
One little turkey flew far away,
But the other . . . (five) decided to stay.

111

Turkey Math Problems (5-0)

Five little turkeys sat in their pen.
"Hide, turkeys, hide!" said the little red hen.
One little turkey hopped out the door,
And when he was gone, there were . . . (four).

Four little turkeys sat in their pen.
"Hide, turkeys, hide!" said the little red hen.
One little turkey flew far away,
But the other . . . (three) decided to stay.

Three little turkeys sat in their pen.
"Hide, turkeys, hide!" said the little red hen.
One little turkey flapped her wings and flew.
And when she was gone, there were . . . (two).

Two little turkeys sat in their pen.
"Hide, turkeys, hide!" said the little red hen.
One little turkey flew far away,
But the last . . . (one) decided to stay.

One little turkey sat in his pen.
"Hide, turkey, hide!" said the little red hen.
The last little turkey flew off toward the sun,
And when he was gone, there were . . . (none)!

Hide turkey, hide!

Turkey Number Sets

1	2
3	4
5	6
7	8
9	10

Thanksgiving Mural

. . . .

Materials:
Butcher paper, scissors, tape, crayons or markers, book about Thanksgiving (see Literature Links suggestions, below)

Preparation:
Cut a long sheet of butcher paper for a mural. Fasten it to the work area by taping the corners down to a table.

Directions:
1. Discuss the fact that the first Thanksgiving was a time when the Pilgrims gave thanks for their first successful harvest. Read a Thanksgiving book, such as *Thanksgiving Day* by Gail Gibbons.
2. Have the children think of something or someone that they are thankful for. It could be a friend, a parent or guardian, a favorite toy or blanket, a skill they've mastered, and so on.
3. Have the children take turns drawing a picture of their chosen person or object on the butcher paper.
4. When all of the children have drawn on the butcher paper, label the mural "Things We Are Thankful For."
5. Post the mural in a school hallway or on a classroom wall.

Option:
Post the children's photographs around the mural, or write the names of all the children as a border for the mural.

Literature Links:
• *Thanksgiving Day* by Gail Gibbons (Holiday House, 1983). This book presents information about the first Thanksgiving and the way the holiday is celebrated today.
• *The First Thanksgiving* by Jean Craighead George, illustrated by Thomas Locker (Philomel, 1993). This beautifully illustrated version of the first Thanksgiving is text heavy, but has abundant factual information.

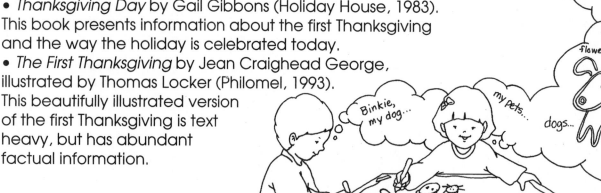

THE BIG FIVE

Materials:
Five Senses patterns (p. 116), crayons

Preparation:
Duplicate a copy of the Five Senses patterns for each child.

Directions:
1. Discuss the five senses with the children. Explain that because of the senses, people can see, hear, smell, taste, and touch.
2. Have the children take turns describing things they've smelled, tasted, touched, seen, and heard.
3. Teach the students The Big Five chant.

> ### The Big Five
> *My five senses make up me:*
> *What I hear and what I see.*
> *What I taste and touch and smell—*
> *My five senses serve me well.*

4. Give each child a copy of the Five Senses patterns. Have children use crayons to draw something they've seen, heard, smelled, tasted, and touched.

Literature Links:
• *My Five Senses* by Aliki (Crowell, 1989).
This simple presentation of the five senses demonstrates some of the ways we use them.
• *My Five Senses* by Margaret Miller (Simon & Schuster, 1994).
This is an introduction to the five senses.

115

Five Senses Patterns

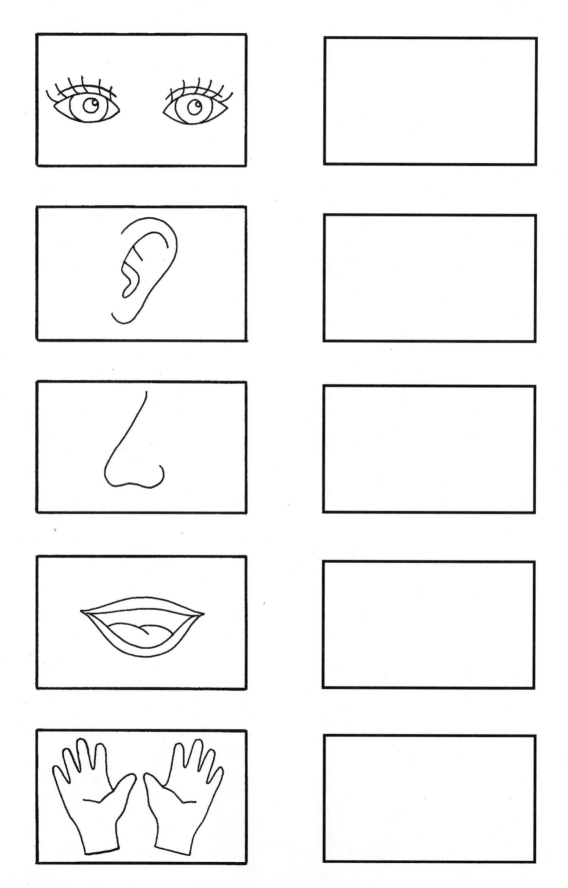

BE-BOP

Materials:
Jazz recordings, cassette player

Preparation:
If possible, read the children the book *Charlie Parker Played Be Bop* before doing this activity. In this book, the writer/illustrator uses pictures and words such as "lollipop," and "chickadee" to make the sounds of a saxophone.

Directions:
1. Discuss the fact that different music makes people feel different ways. Have children share any types of music they like and the way the music makes them feel.
2. Have children sit in a circle and close their eyes.
3. Play a bit of one of the jazz recordings.
4. When you stop the music, have children open their eyes and discuss what they heard. Ask if any of the children thought of specific images when they listened to the music.

Option:
Have children draw pictures of how they felt when the music played. Post the completed drawings on an "Inspired by Jazz" bulletin board.

Literature Link:
• *Charlie Parker Played Be Bop* by Chris Raschka (Orchard, 1992). This book was inspired by "A Night in Tunisia," the so-called be-bop anthem.

The Senses
Science

EYE SEE!

· ·

Materials:
Eye Chart pattern (p. 119), tape

Preparation:
Duplicate and enlarge the Eye Chart pattern. Post the chart low on one wall of the classroom.

Directions:
1. Have children take turns reading the eye chart. They should cover one eye while they read the chart with their other.
2. Ask the children what they see when they look at the eye chart. Acknowledge all answers as acceptable. (After discussing the different things that the children see, you might point out that the eye chart is also the alphabet.)
3. Keep the chart posted in the dress-up corner for children to use when pretending to be doctors.

Eye Chart Pattern

FINGERTIP READING

Materials:
Braille pattern (p. 121), glue, toothpicks

Preparation:
Duplicate a copy of the Braille pattern for each child.

Directions:
1. Explain that people who aren't able to see are called "blind." A blind man named Louis Braille developed a way for blind people to read and write using patterns of raised dots. This is called the Braille System.
2. Give each child a Braille pattern. Have the children observe how the dot patterns represent letters.
3. Provide toothpicks and glue for children to use to fill in the dots on their patterns. They should dab on enough glue to make slightly raised bumps.
4. When the patterns are thoroughly dry, have the children gently touch the pattern that represents each letter. Children can close their eyes as they feel the patterns.

Option:
Have children use the patterns to write their names in Braille. Post these on a "We Read Braille" bulletin board.

Literature Link:
• *Apt. 3* by Ezra Jack Keats (Macmillan, 1971).
On a rainy day, two brothers try to discover who is playing the harmonica they hear in their apartment building.

A ●

B ●
  ●

C ● ●

D ● ●
    ●

E ●
    ●

F ● ●
  ●

G ● ●
  ● ●

H ●
  ● ●

I   ●
  ●

Braille Pattern

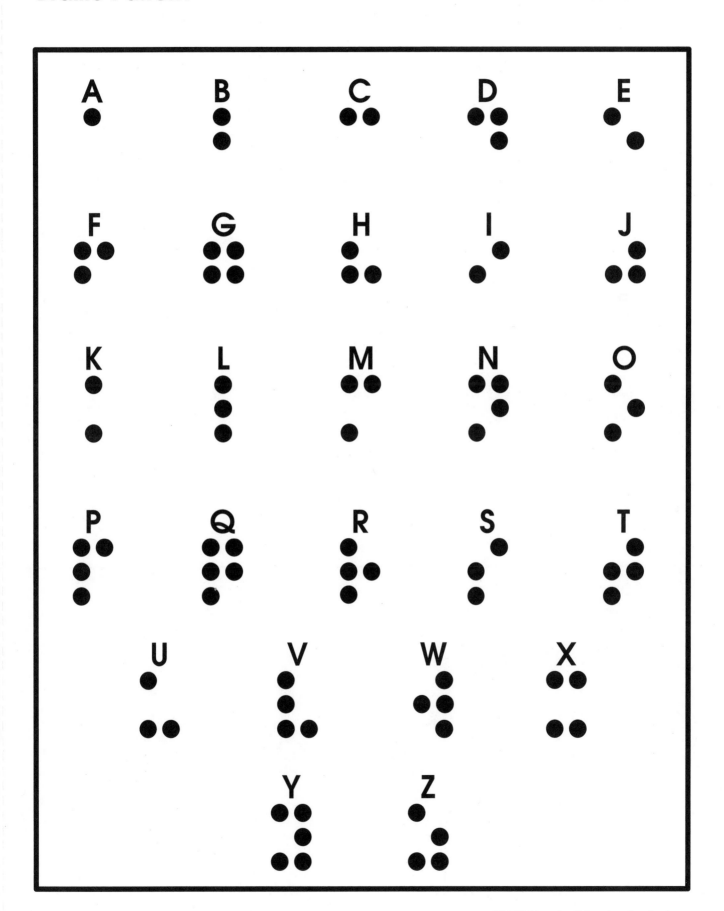

SIGN LANGUAGE

· ·

Materials:
Sign Language pattern (p. 123)

Preparation:
Duplicate a copy of the Sign Language pattern for each child. Duplicate and enlarge one copy of the pattern. Post it on a bulletin board in the classroom.

Directions:
1. Ask the children to cover their ears tightly and say something very quietly to them. Then have them take their hands away and take turns telling everyone what they think was said. Do this several times, saying a different short sentence or word each time.
2. When you have finished, explain that there are people who are unable to hear (or unable to hear well). These people often use sign language to communicate.
3. Give each child a copy of the Sign Language pattern.
4. Have children circle the signs that represent the letters in their names.
5. Children can practice signing their names.

Literature Link:
• *Handsigns* by Kathleen Fain (Chronicle, 1993).
This book presents an animal for each letter of the alphabet, accompanied by the corresponding sign for that letter in American Sign Language.

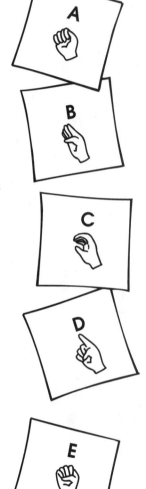

Sign Language Pattern

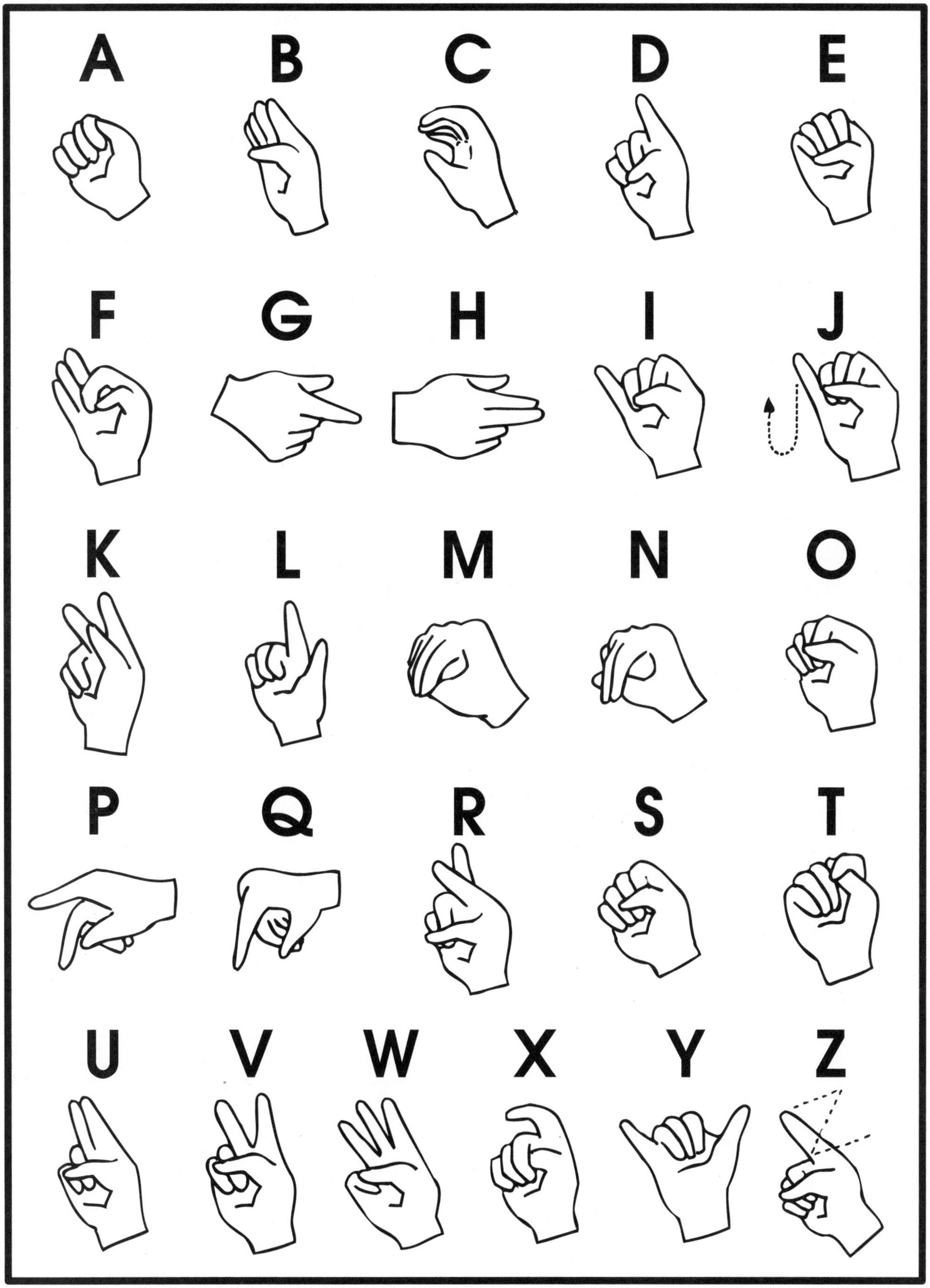

A   B   C   D   E

F   G   H   I   J

K   L   M   N   O

P   Q   R   S   T

U   V   W   X   Y   Z

TASTE TESTING

. . . .

Materials:
Pretzels, lemon wedges, cookies, ice water (or cold juice),
paper plates, cups

Preparation:
Set the above foods out on a table. Make sure there is
enough of each item for each child.

Directions:
1. At snack time, have each child take a pretzel, cookie, and lemon
wedge on a paper plate.
2. Serve ice water or cold juice in cups.
3. Have children take a bite of the different items and describe the
taste: salty, sweet, or sour.
4. Have children decide whether the drink is cold or hot.
5. Discuss the different taste sensations and have children decide
what they like best.

Option:
Substitute a variety of foods for the ones listed above. Raisins are
chewy, chips are salty, cake is sweet, peanut butter is sticky, and so
on. Have children describe the different taste sensations for each
snack tried.

Literature Link:
• *Yummers!* by James Marshall (Houghton Mifflin, 1972).
Emily the pig wants to lose weight, but she can't resist having a few
little snacks.

FINGER COUNTING

Materials:
Hand patterns (p. 126), Finger Math Problems (pp. 127-128), crayons, scissors

Preparation:
Duplicate a copy of the Hand patterns and the Finger Math Problems for each child.

Directions:
1. Give each child a copy of the Hand patterns to cut out. Make sure the children cut out the individual fingers. Children can color the hands if they'd like.
2. As you read the math problems, have children bend one finger over at a time. They can answer the problems by counting the fingers that remain standing.
3. When you have finished the math activity, have children take home the Hand patterns along with copies of the math problems. Children can continue their practice at home.

Literature Link:
• *My Hands Can* by Jean Holzenthaler, illustrated by Nancy Tafuri (Dutton, 1978).
This is a simple book that children can practice reading to themselves.

Hand Patterns

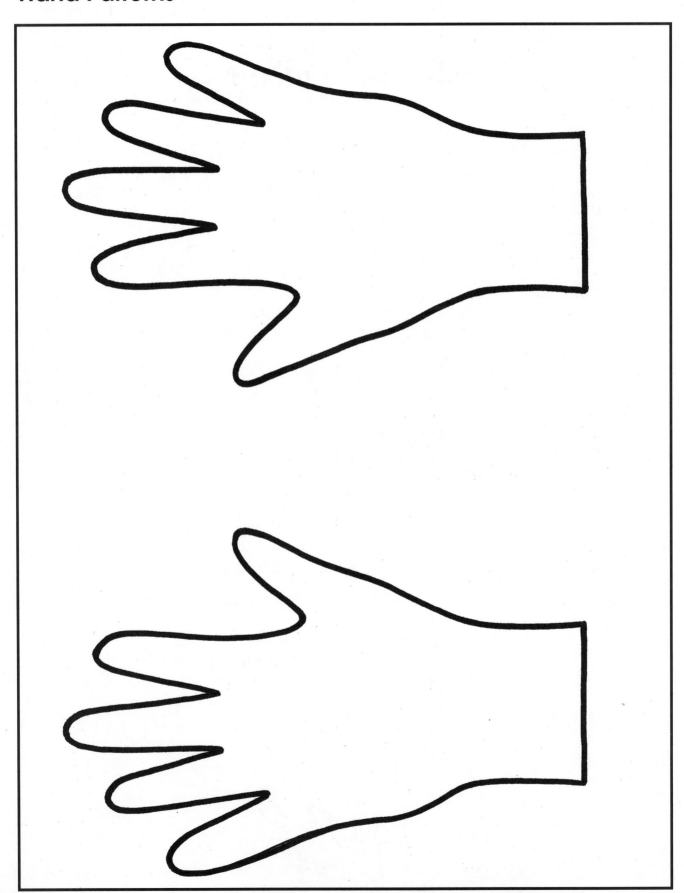

Finger Math Problems (10-5)

This rhyme can be sung to the tune of "I'm a Little Teapot."

I can count my fingers—one to ten.
Ten to one and back again.
Here are all my fingers, standing tall.
Listen, and let's count them all.
(One, two, three, four, five, six, seven, eight, nine, ten!)

My little fingers count to ten.
One bends down to hold a pen.
How many fingers now stand tall?
Listen, and let's count them all.
(One, two, three, four, five, six, seven, eight, nine!)

My little fingers count to nine.
One bends down to draw a line.
How many fingers now stand tall?
Listen, and let's count them all.
(One, two, three, four, five, six, seven, eight!)

My little fingers count to eight.
One bends down to hold a plate.
How many fingers now stand tall?
Listen, and let's count them all.
(One, two, three, four, five, six, seven!)

Seven little fingers count with me!
One bends down to pour some tea.
How many fingers now stand tall?
Listen, and let's count them all.
(One, two, three, four, five, six!)

My little fingers count to six.
One bends down to hold some sticks.
How many fingers now stand tall?
Listen, and let's count them all.
(One, two, three, four, five!)

Finger Math Problems (5-0)

Five little fingers on one hand.
One bends down to hold a rubber band.
How many fingers now stand tall?
Listen, and let's count them all.
(One, two, three, four!)

My little fingers count to four.
One bends down to open the door.
How many fingers now stand tall?
Listen, and let's count them all.
(One, two, three!)

My little fingers count to three.
One bends down to hold a key.
How many fingers now stand tall?
Listen, and let's count them all.
(One, two!)

My little fingers count to two.
One bends down to tie my shoe.
How many fingers now stand tall?
Listen, and let's count them all.
(One!)

My little finger counts to one.
It bends down to hide from the sun.
How many fingers still stand tall?
Listen, and let's count them all.
(None!)

Hand Number Sets

🖐	1	🖐🖐	2
🖐🖐🖐	3	🖐🖐🖐🖐	4
🖐🖐🖐🖐🖐	5	🖐🖐🖐🖐🖐🖐	6
🖐🖐🖐🖐🖐🖐🖐	7	🖐🖐🖐🖐🖐🖐🖐🖐	8
🖐🖐🖐🖐🖐🖐🖐🖐🖐	9	🖐🖐🖐🖐🖐🖐🖐🖐🖐🖐	10

BLINDFOLD DRAWINGS

Materials:
Scarves, white construction paper, felt pens, tape

Preparation:
Make two signs using the white paper. Have one sign read "Eyesight Pictures." Have the other sign read "Blindfolded Pictures." Tape the two signs near each other on a wall.

Directions:
1. Have the children draw pictures of their families.
2. Tape the completed pictures by the sign that reads "Eyesight Pictures."
3. Have the children draw the same family pictures again, but this time while wearing blindfolds.
4. Tape these completed pictures by the sign that reads "Blindfolded Pictures."
5. Have children observe the difference in the pictures. Discuss how much people rely on their eyesight.

Literature Link:
• *Lucy's Picture* by Nicola Moon, illustrated by Alex Ayliffe (Dial, 1995). A young girl creates a special picture that her blind grandfather can "see" with his hands.

PAINTING BY MUSIC

· ·

Materials:
Recorded music, a tape player, butcher paper, paint in tins, paintbrushes, scissors

Preparation:
Cut a mural-length piece of butcher paper. Place paints and paintbrushes on the table.

Directions:
1. Explain that there are many different kinds of music and that the different types can make people feel happy, sad, angry, lonely, and so on.
2. Ask children to share any names of their favorite songs or favorite types of music.
3. Play a variety of music while children work together on a mural.
4. Observe the final picture as a class. Have children discuss what they were feeling when they heard the different types of music played.

Audio Link:
• *Fantasia* (Walt Disney, 1990).
This soundtrack to the famous movie includes the "Nutcracker," "Dance of the Hours," and "Night on Bald Mountain."

RUBBER GLOVE ART

Materials:
Finger-paint paper, tins of paint, one rubber glove per child (Note: Gloves are often available inexpensively in boxes of 50 or more)

Preparation:
None

Directions:
1. Give each child a rubber glove to wear on one hand.
2. Provide paper and tins of paint for children to use to make pictures. Have the children finger-paint with both their rubber-gloved hand and their free hand.
3. Once the children have finished painting, have them discuss the experience of finger-painting using the rubber glove. For example, ask the children whether using gloves was more or less difficult than finger-painting with an ungloved hand.
4. Once the pictures are dry, post them on a bulletin board. Have children try to figure out which strokes were made with bare fingers and which were made with gloved fingers.

Chapter Four
Winter and
Happy Holidays

WINTER WORDS

. . . .

Materials:
Large sheet of white paper, tape, felt pen, easel

Preparation:
Post the white paper on an easel and set it up next to you during circle time.

Directions:
1. Have children brainstorm different things that happen during the winter. (Examples: It gets colder, it snows, frost appears on windows, people wear warmer clothes.)
2. Have students imagine being surrounded by snow.
3. Ask the children to each think of one word describing winter. Give each child a turn to say his or her word. Print each word in large letters on the easel paper.
4. When the paper is covered with descriptive words, post it on a "Winter Words" bulletin board.

Literature Link:
• *The Story of a Boy Named Will Who Went Sledding Down the Hill* by Daniil Kharms (North-South Books, 1993).
Will takes a ride on his sled and picks up a hunter, a dog, a fox, and other creatures on his way down.

ANIMALS, THREE

Materials:
Animal patterns (pp. 136-138), large sheet of paper, glue, colored construction paper, crayons or markers, scissors, tape, black pen

Preparation:
Duplicate the Animal patterns for each child. Duplicate one set for yourself to color and cut out. Divide the white paper into three sections and print the word "Active" at the top of one section, "Hibernators" at the top of the second, and "Resters" at the top of the third. Glue the appropriate eye pattern above each column.

I think that I would be a deer or a rabbit. I like to run and hop.

Winter Animal Facts:
- Active animals, such as foxes and deer, need food and shelter all winter to survive.
- Hibernating animals, such as toads and bats, sleep all winter.
- Animals that rest, such as bears and skunks, can wake up during their winter hibernation, but soon go back to sleep.

Directions:
1. Describe the three kinds of animals in the winter.
2. Post the appropriate animal pictures in each column.
3. Have children color and cut out their own animal patterns.
4. Children can create charts on construction paper by gluing the active animals beneath an open eye, the resters under a half-open eye, and the hibernators under a shut eye.
5. When the children have finished making their charts, ask them to decide which type of winter animals they would most like to be.
6. Give each child a chance to share his or her answer.

Literature Link:
- *Hey! Get Off Our Train!* by John Burningham (Crown, 1989).
A little boy and his toy dog take a train ride through the night. On their journey, they rescue a variety of endangered species.

Active Animals

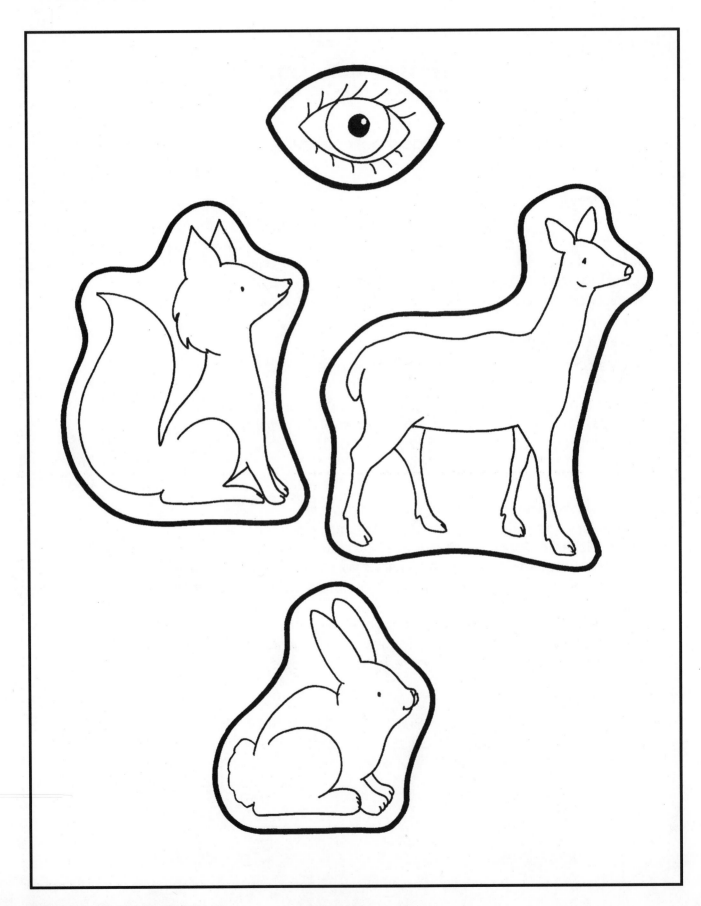

Resters

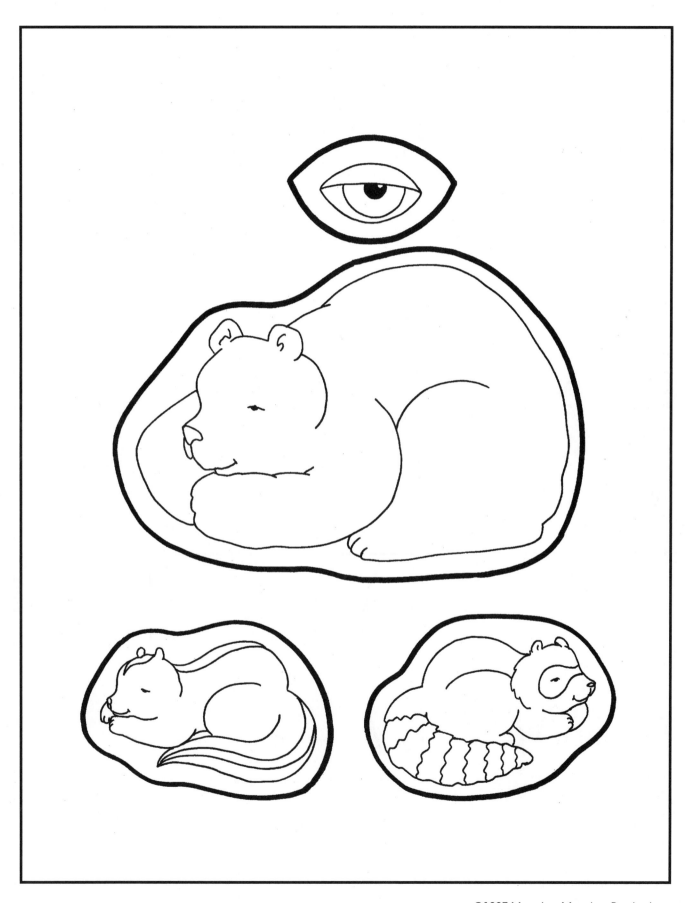

Hibernators

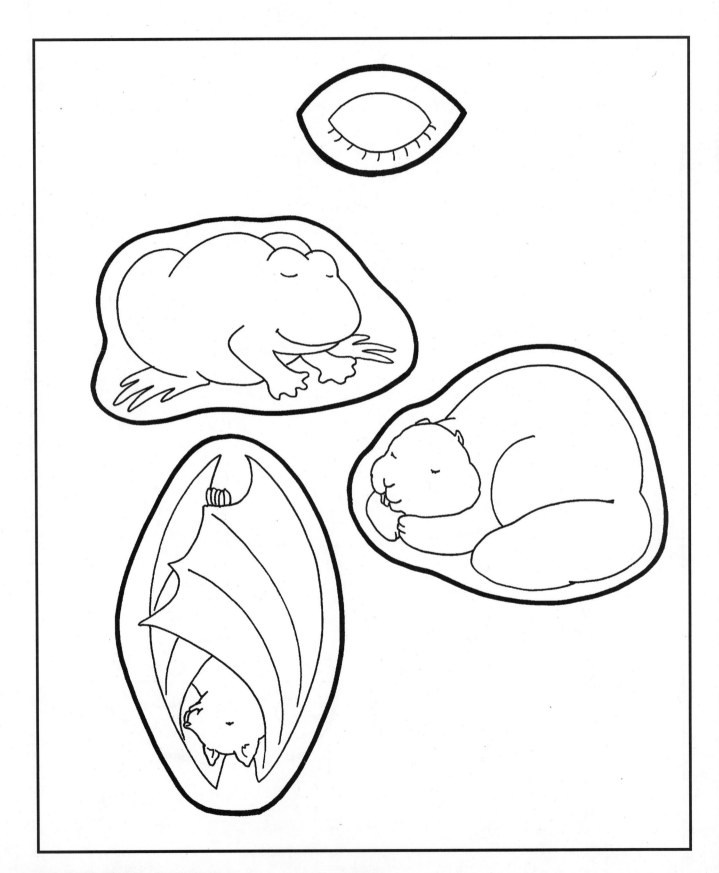

JUMPING MOUSE

· ·

Materials:
Jumping Mouse patterns (p. 140), "Jj" patterns (p. 141), scissors, crayons or markers

Preparation:
Duplicate a Jumping Mouse pattern for each child. Duplicate and enlarge the "Jj" patterns for each child.

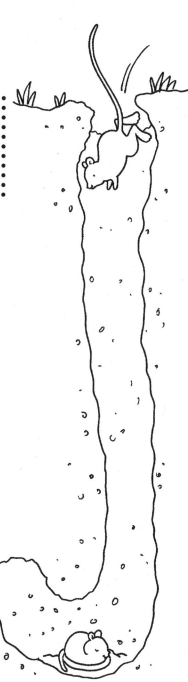

Jumping Mouse Facts:
• The jumping mouse has a tail that is longer than its body.
• In the winter, the jumping mouse hibernates. It digs a tunnel, and then rolls into a little fur ball and falls asleep.

Directions:
1. Have children repeat the sound of the letter "j" with you.
2. Describe the jumping mouse. Have the children roll into tight balls and pretend to be sleeping jumping mice.
3. Wake the children up and pass out the Jumping Mouse patterns for children to color and cut out.
4. Give each child a copy of the enlarged "Jj" pattern. Explain that the top of the J is the ground, and the curve of the J is the tunnel that the jumping mouse has built.
5. Have the children move their jumping mice along the "Jj" patterns. When they move the mice to the bottom of the "J" tunnel, they can glue the mice in place.
6. Post the pictures on a "J Is for Jumping Mice" bulletin board.

Literature Link:
• *Julius, the Baby of the World* by Kevin Henkes (Greenwillow, 1990). Lilly, a mouse, was the best older sister in the world, *before* Julius was born. Once the new baby joins the family, Lilly has her doubts.

Jumping Mouse Patterns

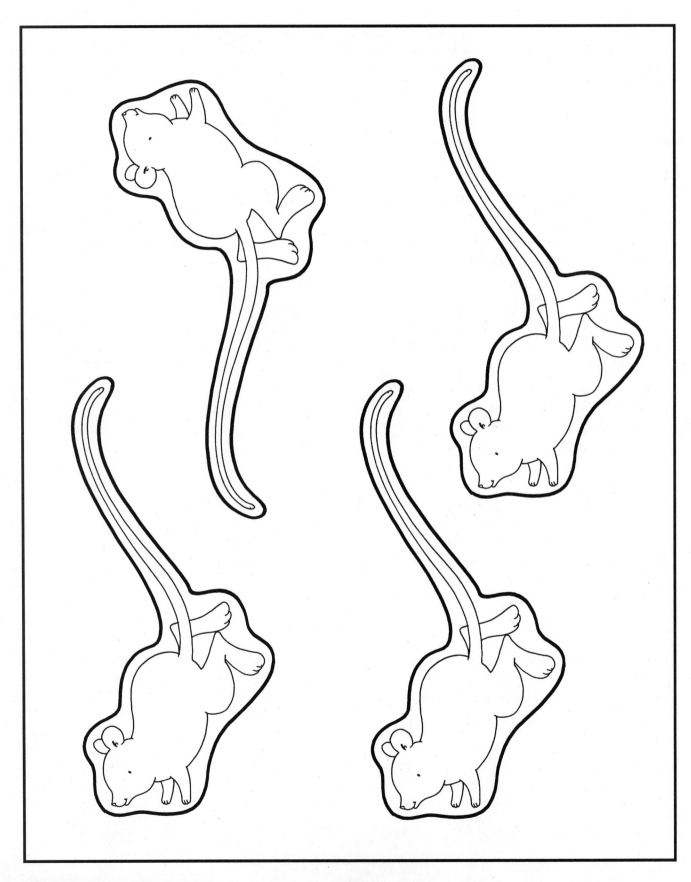

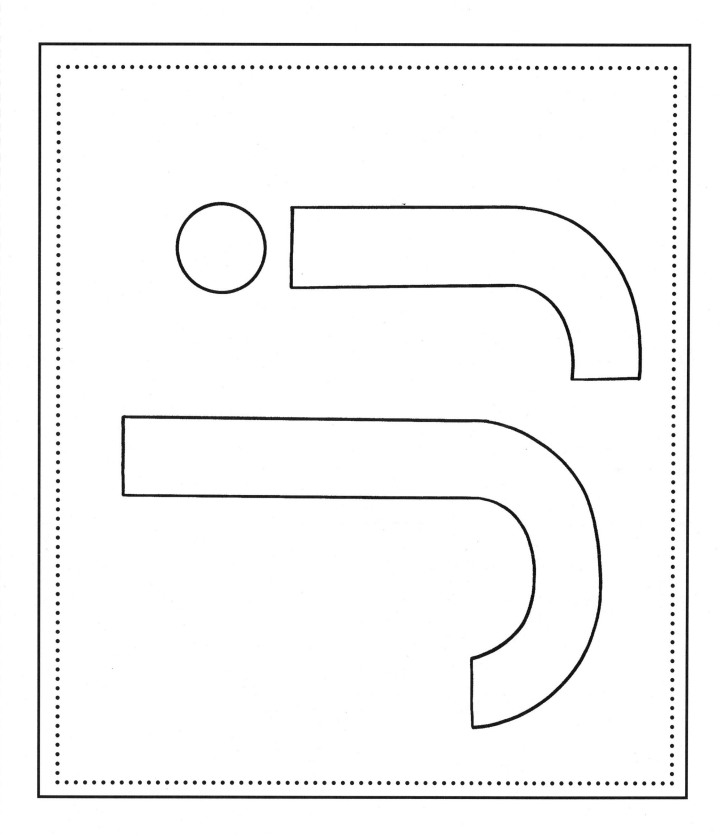

K IS FOR KEY

. . . .

Materials:
Key patterns (p. 143), crayons, scissors, hole punch, long brads (one per child)

Preparation:
Duplicate a copy of the Key patterns for each child.

Directions:
1. Have children repeat the sound of the letter "k" with you.
2. Give each child a copy of the Key patterns to color and cut out.
3. Help the children punch one hole in the top of each Key pattern.
4. Recite the words on the keys with the children. As they recite each word, have them add the key to their "chain." (They can push a brad through the hole in the top of each pattern.)
5. When all of the words have been recited, children can fold their brads over, sealing the keys in place.
6. Send the key rings home with the students for at-home practice.

Option:
Try out these "K" riddles with your kids. Then see if they can think of any to add.
• What kind of key lives in the jungle? A mon<u>key</u>!
• What kind of king do you wear on your foot? A stoc<u>king</u>!
• What kind of kick do you find on a bike? A <u>kick</u>stand!
• What kind of kid do you have in your body? A <u>kid</u>ney!

Literature Link:
• *Alfie Gets in First* by Shirley Hughes (Lothrop, 1981).
Alfie locks his mom and sister outside by accident and can't unlock the door to let them in!

Key Patterns

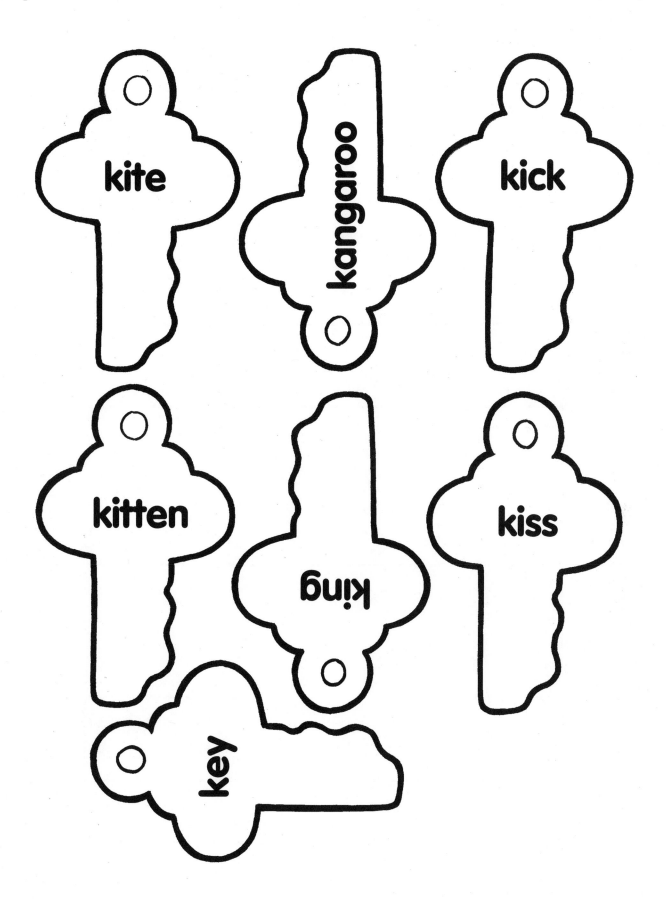

kite

kangaroo

kick

kitten

king

kiss

key

Kk Patterns

L IS FOR LIGHTS

· ·

Materials:
Light patterns (p. 146), glue, colored construction paper, crayons or markers, glitter, scissors

Preparation:
Duplicate a copy of the Light patterns for each child.

Directions:
1. Demonstrate the sound of the letter "l."
2. Discuss the fact that different people celebrate the holidays with different types of lights. At Christmas, many families put lights on their trees. At Hanukkah, families light candles on Menorahs. At Kwanzaa, many families light the candles on their kinara.
3. Give each child a copy of the Light patterns to decorate with glitter, glue, and crayons or markers.
4. Children can cut out the patterns and glue them to sheets of colored construction paper.
5. Post the completed pictures on a "Holiday Lights" bulletin board, or let children take the pictures home.

Literature Links:
• *Celebrating Kwanzaa* by Diane Hoyt-Goldsmith, photographs by Lawrence Migdale (Holiday House, 1993).
• *A Picture Book of Hanukkah* by David A. Adler, illustrated by Linda Heller (Holiday House, 1982).
• *The Trees of Christmas* by Edna Metcalf (Abingdon, 1979).

Light Patterns

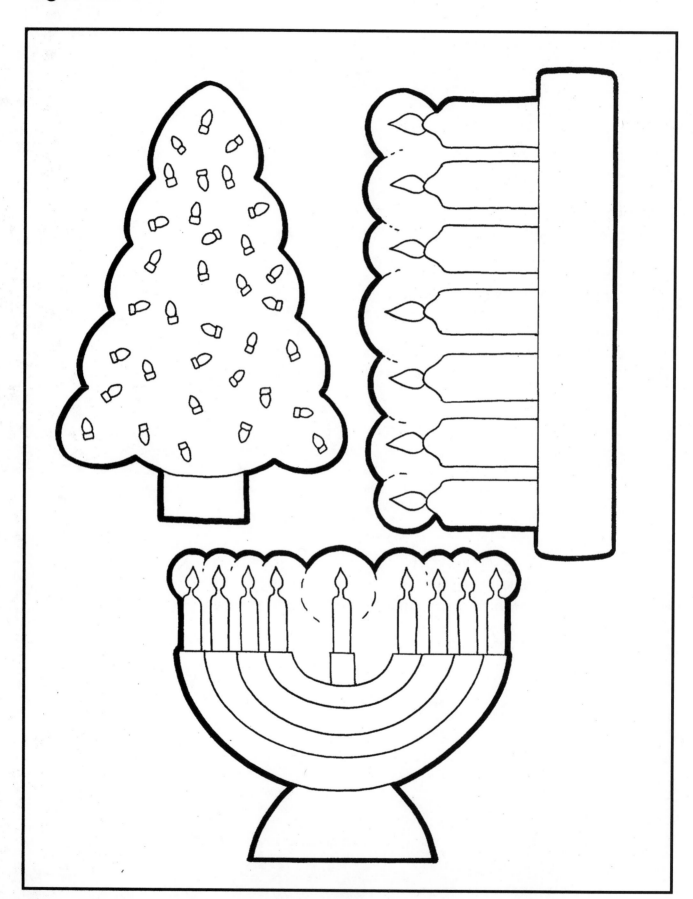

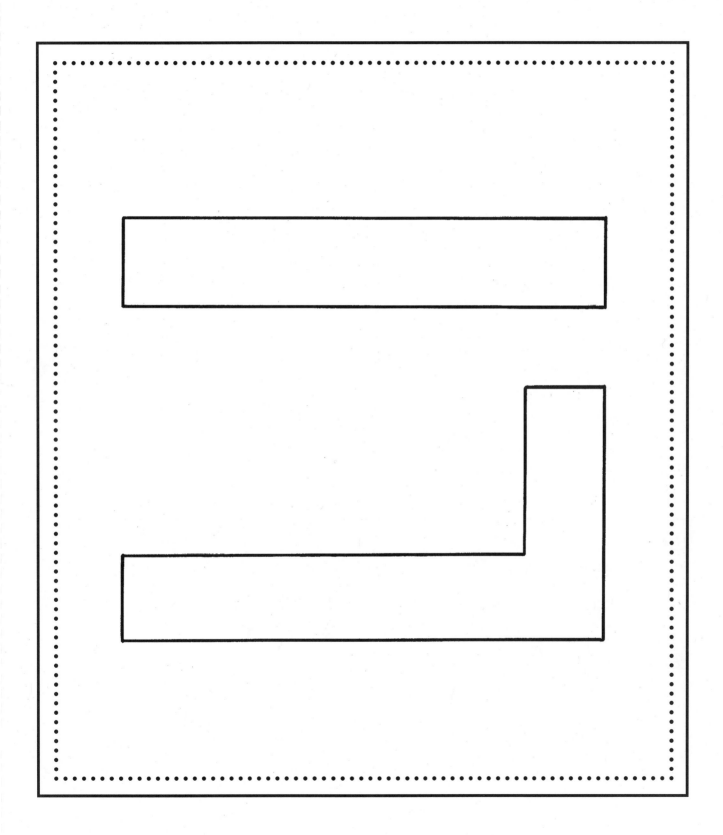

THE CLOUD FAMILY

Materials:
Cloud patterns (p. 149), blue construction paper, scissors, glue

Preparation:
Duplicate a copy of the Cloud patterns for each child. Duplicate and enlarge one copy of the Cloud patterns for yourself.

Cloud Facts:
• There are three main cloud families: cumulus, stratus, and cirrus.
• Cumulus clouds are large puffs of warm air that float upward.
• Stratus clouds look like large flat blankets covering the sky.
• Cirrus clouds can look like donkey tails. They are so high in the sky that the water in them freezes into ice crystals.

Directions:
1. Explain that clouds have names and have the children repeat those names with you.
2. Give each child a copy of the Cloud patterns to cut out and glue to a sheet of blue construction paper. Point out the different types of clouds.
3. Take the children outside and have them look up to the sky.
4. Have the children try to name the types of clouds they see.

Literature Link:
• *Cloudy with a Chance of Meatballs* by Judi Barrett (Atheneum, 1978).
The townspeople of Chew and Swallow enjoy having their meals come down from the sky. But when odd weather hits, it makes for some pretty ridiculous meals!

Cloud Patterns

Cirrus

Cumulus

Stratus

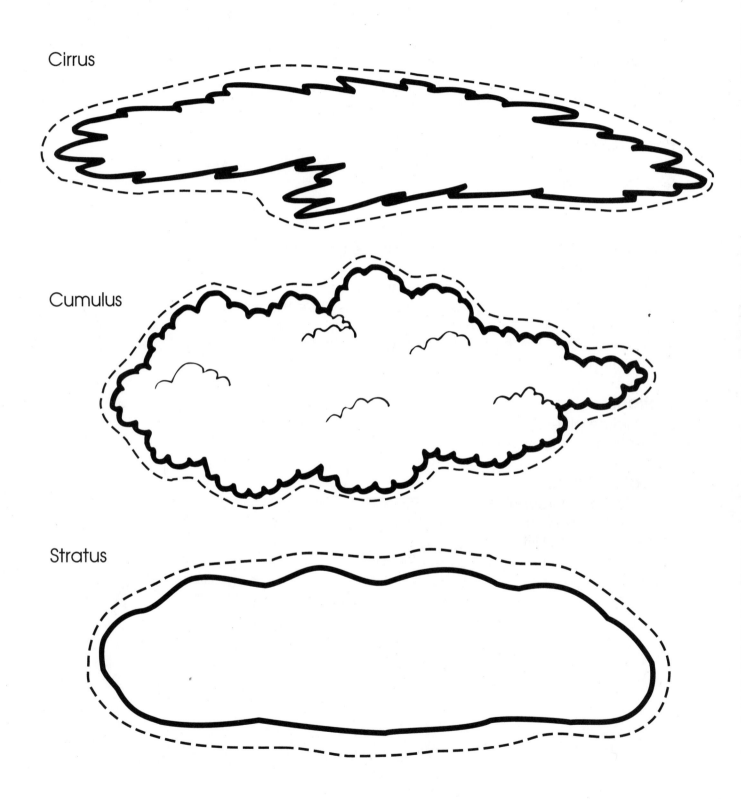

THE SNOWFLAKE MYSTERY

· ·

Materials:
Snowflake patterns (p. 151), Snowflake Math Rap (pp. 152-153), scissors, glitter, glue, envelopes (one per child)

Preparation:
Duplicate a copy of the Snowflake patterns and Snowflake Math Rap for each child.

Directions:
1. Give each child a copy of the Snowflake patterns to cut out and decorate with glitter and glue.
2. Read the Snowflake Math Rap to the children.
3. Have the children manipulate the patterns while the rap is read aloud.
4. Children can store the rap and Snowflake patterns in envelopes for additional at-home practice.

Option:
Let children glue the snowflake patterns onto blue construction paper to make snow scenes.

Literature Link:
• *Madeline's Christmas* by Ludwig Bemelmans (Viking, 1985).
No one is stirring in the house on Christmas Eve except Madeline and a magician. With the magician's help, Madeline runs the school that night when everyone else is sick.

Snowflake Patterns

Snowflake Math Rap (10-5)

Ten little snowflakes caught in a breeze.
One said, "Brrr, I'm starting to freeze!"
This little snowflake flew off to get warm,
But the other . . . (nine) were left in the storm.

Nine little snowflakes up in the sky,
One said, "Look, I know how to fly."
This little snowflake flew far away,
But the other . . . (eight) decided to stay.

Eight little snowflakes dancing around.
One said, "I'm going to check out the ground."
This little snowflake flew down below,
But the other . . . (seven) decided not to go.

Seven little snowflakes caught in the clouds.
One said, "Boy, that thunder is loud!"
This little snowflake left to find a quiet view,
But the other . . . (six) decided not to.

Six little snowflakes were doing cartwheels.
One said, "Now, I know how a Ferris wheel feels!"
This little snowflake left feeling sort of dizzy,
But the other . . . (five) were just getting busy.

Snowflake Math Rap (5-0)

Five little snowflakes were having some fun.
One said, "It's getting late and I'm done."
This little snowflake flew away home,
But the other . . . (four) decided to roam.

Four little snowflakes were doing some tricks.
One said, "I'm off to get my own kicks."
This little snowflake flew toward the sun,
But the other . . . (three) were having too much fun.

Three little snowflakes glittered in the sky.
One felt sad and started to cry.
This little snowflake flew home to mom,
But the other . . . (two) were both getting along.

Two little snowflakes flew around and around.
One said, "I don't want to fall to the ground."
This little snowflake took off on her own,
And the other . . . (one) was left all alone.

One little snowflake out in the blue.
He was all alone and didn't know what to do.
This little snowflake went off to look for friends.
Now he's gone, this is the end!

Snowflake Number Sets

	one		two
	three		four
	five		six
	seven		eight
	nine		ten

154

MY CLOUD BOOK

· ·

Materials:
Cloud Book pattern (p. 156), glue, cotton balls, stapler, yarn and hole punch (optional)

Preparation:
Place glue, paintbrushes, and cotton balls on a table. Duplicate a copy of the Cloud Book pattern for each child.

Directions:
1. Have children glue puffy cotton ball cumulus cloud shapes on the first page of the cloud book.
2. Children can stretch cotton balls to form thin blanket shapes and glue these stratus clouds on the second page.
3. For cirrus clouds, children can stretch cotton balls to form thin curved shapes and glue them on the third page.
4. When all the pages have dried, help children bind their books with a stapler or by punching holes in each page and binding them with yarn.
5. Help children staple the three pages to the cover.
6. Let children read their cloud books aloud.

Literature Link:
• *It Looked Like Spilt Milk* by Charles G. Shaw (HarperFestival, 1947). This creatively illustrated cloud book is available as a board book.

Cloud Book Pattern

My Cloud Book

Look at the cumulus clouds.

Look at the stratus clouds.

Look at the cirrus clouds.

EVENING SNOWFALL

Materials:
Black construction paper, white paint, paintbrushes, a variety of doilies (available at art and craft stores)

Preparation:
Place the black construction paper, white paint, paintbrushes, and doilies on a table.

Directions:
1. Show children the materials they will use to make pictures of an evening snowfall.
2. Demonstrate how to hold a doily on the black paper with one hand and paint over the doily. The entire doily needs to be covered with paint.
3. Encourage children to use different-sized doilies. They can overlap two doilies and paint over them both.
4. When the pictures have dried, post them on a wall.
5. Have children admire the beautiful evening snowfall.

Literature Link:
• *The Snowy Day* by Ezra Jack Keats (Puffin, 1962).
Peter wakes up to discover that it snowed during the night. He puts on his snow suit and goes outside to explore. This is a Caldecott Award book.

©1997 Monday Morning Books, Inc.

SNOW HOUSE

. . . .

Materials:
Sugar cubes, glue, paintbrushes, paper plates

Preparation:
Place the sugar cubes, glue, paintbrushes, and paper plates on a table.

Directions:
1. Explain that in Japan people celebrate the snowfall with a Snow Festival. During the Snow Festival, children build snow houses to sit and sing in.
2. Demonstrate how to build a "snow" house. Children can use a paintbrush to brush glue on sugar cubes. They can then glue the sugar cubes together to make snow houses.
3. Encourage the children to be imaginative. A snow house can be any shape or size.
4. Place the dry snow houses on a table labeled "Super Snow Houses."

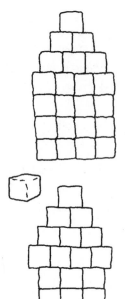

Option:
Build a large snow house by draping a sheet over a clothesline. Children can sit under the sheet and pretend to be inside a giant snow house.

Literature Link:
• *A House Is a House for Me* by Mary Ann Hoberman (Viking, 1978). This book shows houses for various animals and objects. A chicken's house is a coop, a hand's house is a glove, an ant's house is a hill, and a potato's house is a pot!

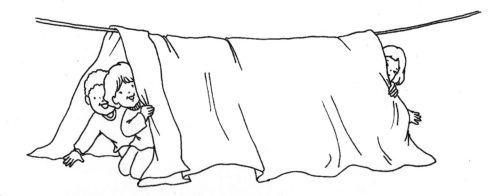

SNOWFLAKE CONCENTRATION

Materials:
Snowflake patterns (p. 151), scissors, crayons or markers, clear
Contac paper or laminator (optional)

Preparation:
For each set, make two copies of the Snowflake patterns. Color the
two copies exactly alike and cut the cards out. Laminate or cover
with clear Contac paper. (This will protect the cards and make
them last longer.) Teach children how to play the game of Concentration.

Directions to Play:
1. All of the cards are spread out face down.
2. The first child turns two cards over.
3. If the cards match, the child keeps the pair and goes again.
4. If the cards don't match, the child turns the cards face down,
and the next child takes a turn.
5. Play continues until all of the cards are matched.

Literature Link:
• *Harold at the North Pole: A Christmas Journey with the Purple
Crayon* by Crocket Johnson (Reader's Digest, 1958).
Harold sets off in his woolen hat and mittens to visit the North Pole.

HOLIDAY GRAB BAG

. . . .

Materials:
Scarf, pillowcase, variety of small objects that represent the holidays
(wrapping paper, a bow, a candy cane, a Menorah, an ornament,
a cookie cutter, a candle, and so on)

Preparation:
Collect the small objects and place them in the pillowcase.

Directions:
1. Sit with the children on the rug. Display the holiday "grab bag."
2. Start the game by blindfolding a child with the scarf. (Children
can close their eyes if they don't want to be blindfolded.)
3. Have the child reach into the bag and pull out an item.
4. This child then feels the object and tries to guess what it is.
5. After three guesses, if the child doesn't know, have the other
children shout out the answer. The next child takes a turn.
6. When all of the children have had a turn, place the objects on a
small table. Label the table with a sign that reads "Objects That
Represent the Holidays."

Literature Link:
• *The Velveteen Rabbit* by Margery Williams (Camelot, 1975).
The best gift of all, according to the toys in the nursery, is to be real.

THE ALPHABET GIFT

Materials:
Shoe box with lid, knife (for adult use only), tape, wrapping paper, scissors, white paper, felt pen

Preparation:
Cut white paper into small squares. Print a different alphabet letter on each square, and place the squares in the box. Wrap up the shoe box with the lid on. Cut a hole in the center of the lid, big enough for a child's hand to fit through.

Directions:
1. Discuss the fact that during the holiday season many people exchange gifts.
2. Have the children sit in a circle. Display the Alphabet Gift Box. Explain that there are many imaginary gifts inside this box, each one beginning with a letter of the alphabet.
3. Teach the children the ABC Chant.

> ### ABC Chant
> *A, B, C, D, E, F, G.*
> *What in the world did you get for me?*
> *An A, a B, a candy cane C?*
> *Pull out a gift and what do you see?*

4. Pass the Alphabet Gift Box to a child. This child pulls a square from the box and then thinks of a gift that begins with the letter on the square. (The remaining children can offer suggestions, if needed.)
5. Repeat the chant and pass the box to the next child. This child pulls out a letter and tries to think of a gift.
6. Continue with the game until each child has had a turn.

Literature Link:
• *Mr. Rabbit and the Lovely Present* by Charlotte Zolotow, illustrated by Maurice Sendak (Harper & Row, 1962).
A little girl goes on a search for the perfect gift for her mother.

HUGE HAILSTONES

Materials:
Sheets of scrap paper, large grapefruit, paper bags (one per child)

Preparation;
Crunch sheets of scrap paper together to form "hailstones." Use one sheet to form small hailstones, two sheets to form medium-sized hailstones, or many sheets to form large hailstones. Place sheets of scrap paper on a table.

Hailstone Facts:
• Hailstones begin as tiny crystals of ice.
• Drops of water begin to stick to the ice crystals, making them heavier.
• The heavy crystals swirl inside the clouds until many layers of water stick to them.
• The heavy ice crystals fall to the ground as hailstones.

Directions:
1. Display the various paper hailstones.
2. Explain that hailstones can come in many different shapes: cones, curved bananas, or even mushrooms.
3. Have children make paper hailstones. They can form round shapes or try the shapes mentioned above.
4. When the children have finished, ask the question, "How large do you think the largest hailstone was?" Display the grapefruit. A hailstone this large landed in Nebraska.
5. Let children take their hailstones home in paper bags.

REINDEER RHYMES

Materials:
Reindeer patterns (p. 164), Reindeer Math Rhyme (pp. 165-166), crayons or markers, scissors, envelopes (one per child)

Preparation:
Duplicate a copy of the Reindeer patterns and the Reindeer Math Rhyme for each child.

Directions:
1. Give each child a copy of the Reindeer patterns to color and cut out.
2. Read the Reindeer Math Rhyme to the children.
3. Have the children manipulate the patterns while the rhyme is read aloud.
4. Children can store the patterns and rhymes in envelopes for additional at-home practice.

Option:
Sing a round of "Rudolph the Red-nosed Reindeer" before doing this activity. Remind children of the line about the "reindeer games." Ask children to share their ideas of what reindeer games might be.

Literature Link:
• *The Wild Christmas Reindeer* by Jan Brett (Putnam, 1990).
After a few false starts, Teeka discovers the best way to get Santa's reindeer ready for Christmas Eve.

Reindeer Patterns

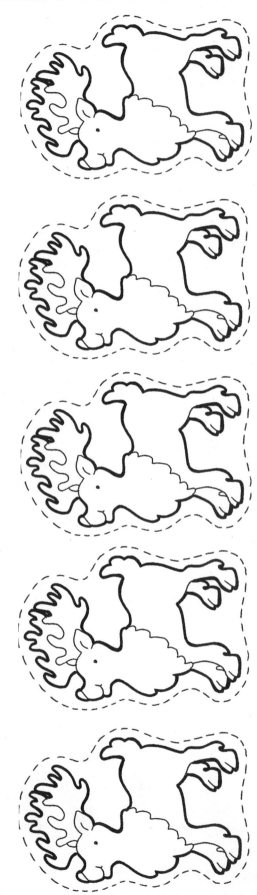
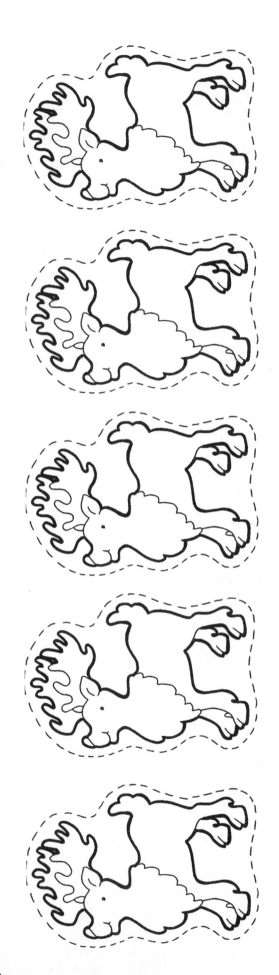

Reindeer Math Rhyme (10-5)

Ten reindeer were playing out in the snow,
They played hide-and-seek.
Reindeer love that, you know.
One little reindeer hid behind a pine,
And with him hiding, that left . . . (nine).

Nine reindeer were playing out in the snow.
They played a game of baseball.
Reindeer love that, you know.
One little reindeer slid way past home plate,
And with him gone, that left . . . (eight).

Eight reindeer were playing out in the snow.
They played Duck, Duck, Goose!
Reindeer love that, you know.
One reindeer gave another a push,
And the other . . . (seven) left him in the mush!

Seven reindeer were playing out in the snow.
They played pick-up-sticks.
Reindeer love that, you know.
One reindeer lost all of his sticks,
And with him out, that left . . . (six).

Six reindeer were playing out in the snow.
They played a game of tag.
Reindeer love that, you know.
One reindeer ran right into a beehive,
And with him gone, that left . . . (five).

Reindeer Math Rhyme (5-0)

Five reindeer were playing out in the snow.
They played Go Fish,
Reindeer love that, you know.
One reindeer didn't want to play anymore,
And with him gone, that left . . . (four).

Four reindeer were playing out in the snow.
They played football.
Reindeer love that, you know.
One reindeer decided to be referee,
And with him out, that left . . . (three).

Three reindeer were playing out in the snow.
They played Marco Polo.
Reindeer love that, you know.
One reindeer decided that she was through,
And with her gone, that left . . . (two).

Two reindeer were playing out in the snow.
They played a game of Bingo.
Reindeer love that, you know.
One reindeer decided it wasn't that much fun,
And with him gone, that left . . . (one).

One reindeer was playing out in the snow.
He was all by himself.
Reindeer hate that, you know.
That reindeer decided to go and find a friend,
And with him gone, this is the end!

Reindeer Number Sets

🦌	1	🦌🦌	2
🦌🦌🦌🦌	3	🦌🦌🦌🦌	4
🦌🦌🦌🦌🦌	5	🦌🦌🦌🦌🦌🦌	6
🦌🦌🦌🦌🦌🦌🦌	7	🦌🦌🦌🦌🦌🦌🦌🦌	8
🦌🦌🦌🦌🦌🦌🦌🦌🦌	9	🦌🦌🦌🦌🦌🦌🦌🦌🦌🦌	10

167

JUMPING REINDEER

. . . .

Materials:
Ball, white construction paper, tape, felt pen

Preparation:
Print the names of Santa's reindeer on a sheet of white paper. Tape the paper to a wall.

Directions:
1. Sit with the children in a circle and point to the names of the nine reindeer. Count them and then say their names.
2. Teach children the Reindeer Chant. Clap to establish a rhythm.

> **The Reindeer Chant**
> *Jump, reindeer, jump,*
> *At Santa's command.*
> *You can hear jolly Santa*
> *Throughout the land.*
> *Get ready, get set,*
> *To fly, fly, fly.*
> *Jump, reindeer, jump,*
> *Jump up, jump high.*

one, two, three, ...

3. Choose a child to stand in the center of the circle. This child names one of the reindeer to train. Give this child the ball.
4. Have the child bounce the ball until he or she misses a beat. Everyone can count as the ball hits the ground. Mark the number under the name of the chosen reindeer.
5. When the child misses, he or she rolls the ball to another child who becomes the next trainer. Repeat the chant and play again.

Note:
With a large group of children, play this game over a few days. Display how many jumps each reindeer made with a graph at the end of the activity.

Literature Link:
• *Reindeer* by Emery Bernhard (Holiday House, 1994).
This is a nonfiction reindeer resource.

DANCING SNOWMEN

Materials:
Snowman pattern (p. 170), scissors, crayons, yarn, hole punch, recorded music and player (optional)

Preparation:
Duplicate a copy of the Snowman pattern for each child. Cut two arm-length pieces of yarn for each child. Place the crayons, scissors, and yarn at the table.

Directions:
1. Give each child a sheet of copy of the Snowman pattern.
2. Demonstrate how to fold the pattern in thirds with the snowman on the front.
3. Show children how to cut out the snowmen, working slowly and staying on the lines.
4. Children can unfold their papers to reveal their snowmen.
5. Let children decorate the snowmen using crayons.
6. Let the children take turns punching holes in the hat of the snowman on each end of their chain.
7. Help children thread a string of yarn through the holes and tie at the top.
8. Hang the snowmen around the room. If you hang them near an open window, they will dance in the breeze.

Option:
Sit with the children on the rug. Play holiday music while the children hold their lines of snowmen by the strings and make them dance.

Literature Link:
• *One Snowman* by M.B. Goffstein (Harper and Row, 1986).
A lonely snowman gets a wife in this beautifully illustrated book.

Snowman Pattern

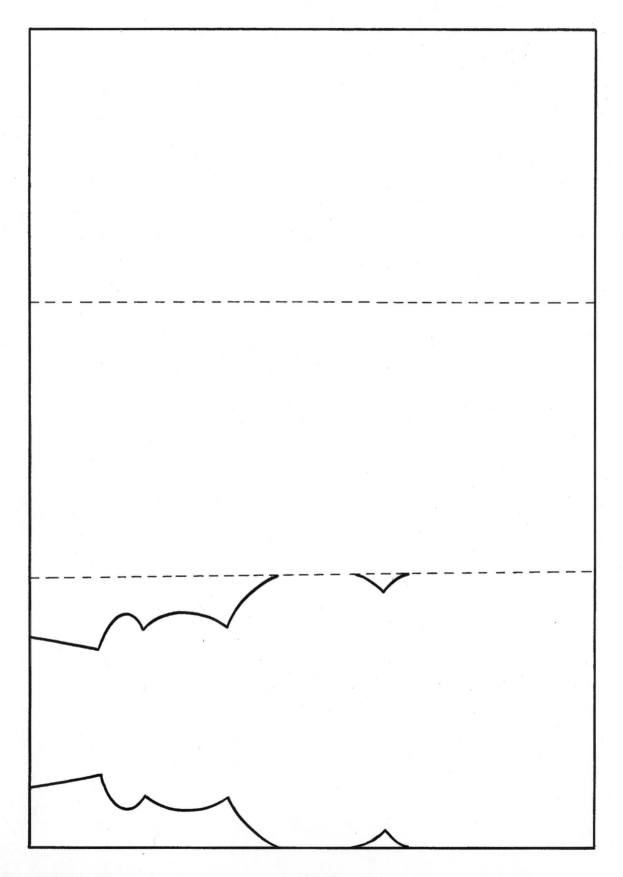

Chapter Five
New Year and Famous Artists

JANUARY FIRST

. . . .

Materials:
Month patterns (p. 173), scissors, crayons or markers

Preparation:
Duplicate and enlarge the Month patterns.
Color and cut out.

Directions:
1. Explain that people celebrate New Year's Eve because it is the end of one year and the beginning of another.
2. Choose 12 children to represent the 12 months of the year. Have these children stand in a straight line.
3. Give each child a month card to hold, from January through December.
4. Point to the child holding January, and explain that January is the first month of a new year.
5. Beginning with January, read the name of each month.
6. At December, explain that this is the final month of the year. People go to sleep on the last day of December and wake up in the new year.
7. Point to January and have the children yell, "Happy New Year!"

Literature Link:
• *Little Sister and the Month Brothers* retold by Beatrice Schenk de Regniers, illustrated by Margo Tomes (Clarion, 1976).
This Slavic story tells of a meeting between a young woman and the 12 month brothers who are in charge of the seasons.

Month Patterns

January

July

February

August

March

September

April

October

May

November

June

December

CHINESE NEW YEAR

• •

Materials:
Dragon pattern (p. 175), globe, red and yellow crepe paper, pennies, tissue paper, crayons, scissors, pipe cleaners

Preparation:
Duplicate a copy of the Dragon pattern for each child. Cut the tissue paper into small squares. Make two colored squares for each child.

Chinese New Year's Celebration Facts:
• In China, people clean house before the new year comes.
• Families visit friends to say goodbye to the old year.
• Money is wrapped in colorful paper and given to children.
• People decorate their homes with paper flowers.
• Many people carry a large paper dragon in the streets.

Directions:
1. Let the children help you find China on the globe. Explain that you will be discussing New Year's celebrations in China.
2. Shake hands with the children and say goodbye to the old year.
3. Have each child wrap a penny in a colored square of paper and put the penny in his or her pocket (or cubby).
4. Show children how to make simple flowers from tissue paper.
5. Give each child a Dragon pattern to decorate with crayons.
6. Post the completed dragons on a "Gung Hay Fat Choy!" bulletin board. This saying means "wishing you good fortune and happiness." Decorate the board with a paper flower border.

Literature Link:
• *Chinese New Year* by Tricia Brown, photographs by Fran Ortiz (Henry Holt, 1987).
This informative book has many wonderful pictures.

Dragon Pattern

ETHIOPIAN CELEBRATIONS

Materials:
Globe, green and brown pipe cleaners, scissors, colored tissue paper scraps, glue

Preparation:
Set the pipe cleaners, tissue paper scraps, and glue on a table.

Ethiopian New Year's Celebration Facts:
- Girls in Ethiopia make flower bouquets and sing from house to house.
- Ethiopian boys gather bundles of branches and make a fire in the evening. They also sing songs at people's houses.

Directions:
1. Have the children help you locate Ethiopia on the globe.
2. Discuss the New Year's celebration in Ethiopia.
3. Children can tear or crumple pieces of tissue paper to form a variety of flower shapes. These can be glued onto green pipe cleaners to make flower bouquets.
4. Children can also glue brown pipe cleaners together for firewood. They can also add tissue paper blossoms on the branches.

Literature Link:
- *The Perfect Orange: A Tale from Ethiopia* by Frank P. Araujo, illustrated by Xiao Jun Li (Rayve Productions, 1994).

"M" IS FOR MOTHER GOOSE

Materials:
Mother Goose Month Rhymes (p. 178), Mother Goose pattern (p. 179), feathers (available at arts and crafts stores), glue, crayons or markers

Preparation:
Duplicate a copy of the Mother Goose pattern for each child.

Directions:
1. Have the children repeat the sound of the letter "m" with you.
2. Teach the children the famous Mother Goose rhyme. Or duplicate the Mother Goose Month Rhymes to read aloud.

Old Mother Goose

*Old Mother Goose,
When she wanted to wander,
Would fly through the air
On a very fine gander.*

*Old Mother Goose had a young lad,
He was not very good
Nor yet very bad.*

*She sent him to market
A live goose he bought:
"Here! Mother," says he,
"It will not go for naught."*

*And Old Mother Goose,
The goose saddled soon,
And mounting its back,
Flew up to the moon.*

---

3. After you've said the rhyme once, point out the words that start with "m" in the poem: mother, market, mounting, and moon.
4. Give each child a copy of the Mother Goose pattern to decorate using feathers, glue, and crayons or markers.
5. Post the completed pictures on a "Marvelous Mother Goose" bulletin board.

Literature Link:
• *Mother Goose: The Classic Volland Edition*, illustrated by Frederick Richardson (Hubbard Press, 1971).
This is a beautifully illustrated edition of classic Mother Goose.

Mother Goose Month Rhymes

Thirty days hath September,
April, June, and November,
All the rest have thirty-one,
Except February which has
  twenty-eight,
In Leap Year, twenty-nine.

January brings the snow,
Makes our feet and fingers glow.

February brings the rain,
Thaws the frozen lake again.

March brings breezes, loud
  and shrill,
To stir the dancing daffodil.

April brings the primrose sweet,
Scatters daisies at our feet.

May brings flocks of pretty lambs,
Skipping by their fleecy dams.

June brings tulips, lilies, roses,
Fills the children's hands with posies.

Hot July brings cooling showers,
Apricots and gillyflowers.

August brings the sheaves of corn;
Then the harvest home is borne.

Warm September brings the fruit;
Sportsmen then begin to shoot.

Fresh October brings the pheasant;
Then to gather nuts is pleasant.

Dull November brings the blast;
Then the leaves are whirling fast.

Chill December brings the sleet,
Blazing fire, and Christmas treat.

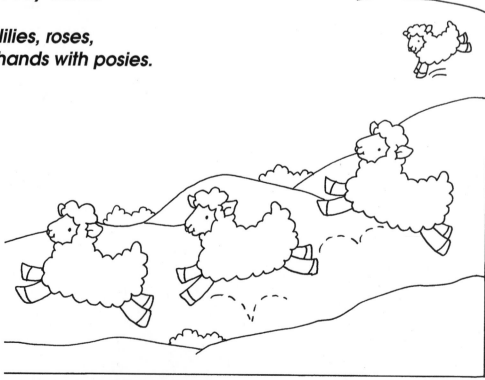

Mother Goose Pattern

Mm Patterns

WHAT'S NEW?

• •

Materials:
New Year pattern (p. 182), felt pens, butcher paper, scissors, tape

Preparation:
Duplicate a copy of the New Year pattern for each child. Tape a large sheet of butcher paper on a wall. At the top of the paper, print: "A new year can bring...."

Directions:
1. Practice the sound of the letter "n" with the children.
2. Explain that a new year can bring many new things. Have the children brainstorm some of these new things, perhaps a new toy, a new friend, a new class, or a new skill.
3. Repeat the words on the butcher paper, then have the children say them with you.
4. Ask for a volunteer to read the words and finish the sentence. Write the ending of the sentence on the butcher paper. (For example, if the child says, "A new year can bring a new toy," write "a new toy" on the butcher paper.
5. Choose another child to read the words and finish the sentence.
6. When all of the children have had a turn, give each child a copy of the New Year pattern.
7. The children can draw pictures that finish the sentence.
8. Post the completed papers on a "New Year Brings...." bulletin board.

Literature Link:
• *Goodbye Old Year, Hello New Year* by Frank Modell (Greenwillow, 1984).
Marvin and Milton want to celebrate the coming of the new year, but they fall asleep before midnight.

©1997 Monday Morning Books, Inc.

New Year Pattern

A New Year can bring...

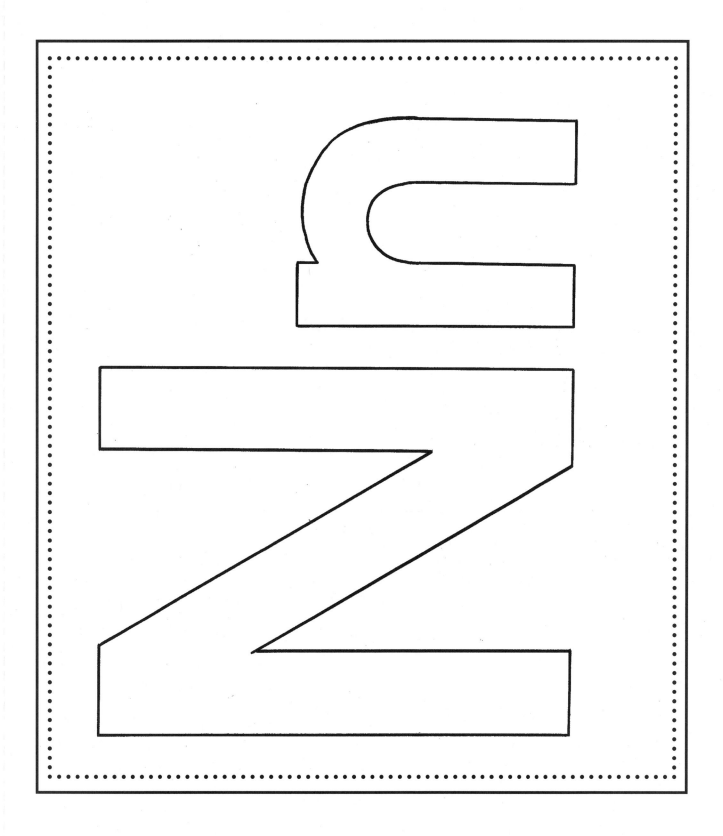

"O," My Darlin'

. . . .

Materials:
"Oo" patterns (p. 185), orange crayons, Cheerios, glue

Preparation:
Duplicate a copy of the "Oo" patterns for each child.

Directions:
1. Have the children practice the sound of the letter "o" with you.
2. Explain that the old year is over and the new year is starting.
3. Teach the "Oh, My Darlin' O" song, to the tune of "Clementine."

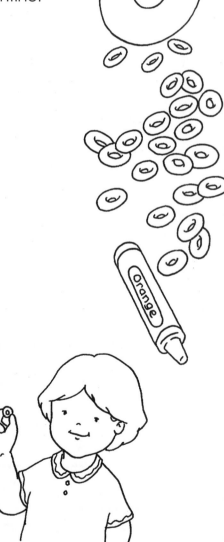

> ### Oh, My Darlin' O
> *Oh, my darlin', oh, my darlin',*
> *Oh I love the letter o.*
> *O is round and o is special,*
> *Oatmeal begins with o.*
>
> *O's a letter,*
> *In the middle of the alphabet, my friend,*
> *It's a very special letter,*
> *And it comes right after n.*
>
> *O's a vowel.*
> *It's important.*
> *You can find it if you look.*
> *It's in words like love and open,*
> *And it's even twice in book!*
>
> **(Repeat first verse)**

4. Give each child a copy of the "Oo" patterns to decorate using Cheerios, glue, and orange crayons.

Literature Link:
• *Over, Under and Through and Other Spatial Concepts* by Tana Hoban (Macmillan, 1973).

Oo Patterns

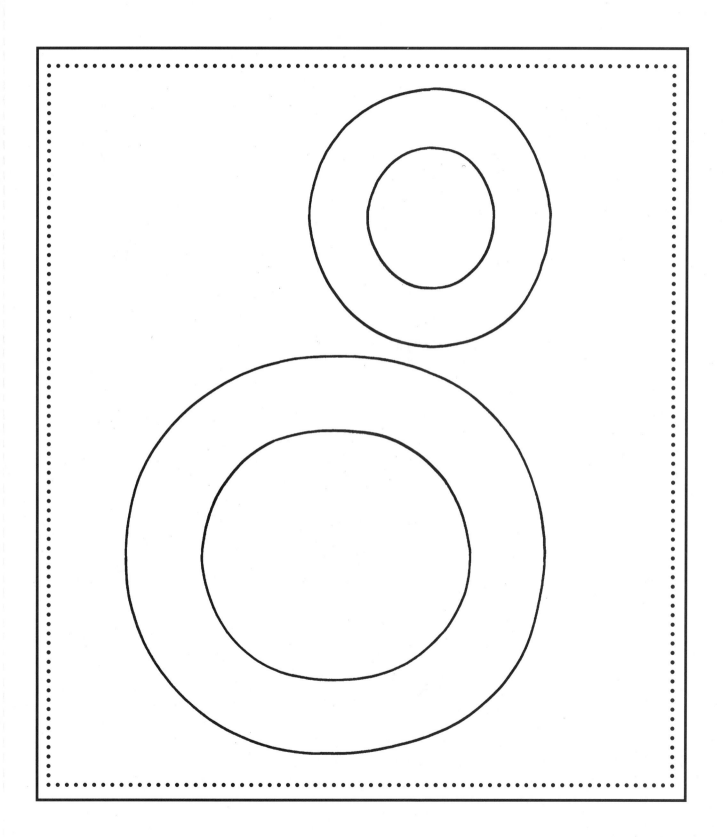

FROSTY DAYS

Materials:
Clean tin can, crushed ice, rock salt, glass, water

Preparation:
Remove the label from the can.

Directions:
1. Let the children help you fill the tin can with alternating layers of crushed ice and rock salt.
2. While the can sits, have children describe places where they have seen frost.
3. Have the children observe how the water vapor changes into ice crystals.
4. Fill a glass with ice water and have the children compare the can and the glass. Children can observe the differences between the outside of the can and the glass of water.

ORDER OF MONTHS

Materials:
Months Rhyme (p. 188), Months and Numbers patterns (p. 189), crayons or markers, glue, colored construction paper, scissors

Preparation:
Duplicate a copy of the Months Rhyme and the Months and Numbers patterns for each child.

Directions:
1. Give each child a copy of the Months and Numbers patterns to cut out. Each month should remain with its number. The numbers will help the children arrange the months in the correct order.
2. Teach the children the Months Rhyme.
3. Have children organize their patterns so that January comes first and December comes last. (Help children who need it.)
4. Let children glue their patterns onto construction paper in the proper order. Children can use crayons to decorate the patterns.

Literature Link:
• *The Months of the Year* by Paul Hughes (Garrett, 1989).
This teacher resource presents a variety of songs, stories, festivals, and traditions about the months of the year from all over the world.

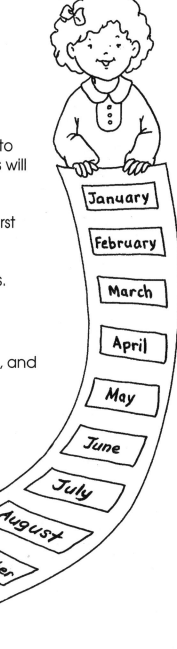

Months Rhyme

New Year's Day is lots of fun.
January's number one.

In February, there's lots to do.
This is month number two.

In March, leaves grow on the trees.
This is month number three.

April trees have buds galore.
This is month number four.

May bees buzz within their hives.
This is month number five.

June is filled with cheeps from chicks.
This is month number six.

July's sun beams in the heavens.
This is month number seven.

In August, the sun stays out late.
This is month number eight.

In September, school is fine.
This is month number nine.

In October, Halloween's here again.
This is month number ten.

In November relatives drive in.
This is month number eleven.

December gifts are on the shelves.
This is month number twelve.

Months and Numbers Patterns

January	1	July	7
February	2	August	8
March	3	September	9
April	4	October	10
May	5	November	11
June	6	December	12

THAILAND NEW YEAR

. . . .

Materials:
Globe, uncooked rice, small paper cups (one per child), tissue paper, tape or ribbons, scissors

Preparation:
Cut tissue paper into large squares. Make one square for each child. Pour a small amount of rice into a paper cup for each child.

Thailand New Year's Celebrations Facts:
- There are street parades.
- People wade in ponds and rivers and dump buckets of water on each other for surprise showers.
- Pet birds and fish are set free.
- People wrap up rice and give it away as gifts.

Directions:
1. Have children help you locate Thailand on the globe. Explain that Thailand's New Year celebration begins on April 13th. It is called the Water Festival. Explain that Thailand has very hot weather and water is extremely important to the Thai people.
2. Children can wrap the pieces of tissue around their cups, covering the tops. Show them how to tape the tissue in place. They can also use ribbons to fasten the tissue.
3. Children can give away their decorated rice cups as gifts.

Option:
Provide sticky stars and glitter for children to use to further decorate their tissue wrapping.

Literature Link:
- *The Paper-Flower Tree: A Tale from Thailand* by Jacqueline Ayer (Harcourt, 1962).
This is the magical story of a little girl who plants a bead and grows a paper-flower tree.

WATER FESTIVAL ART

Materials:
White construction paper, felt pens, blue powdered tempera and water or blue watercolors, paintbrushes, newsprint, Thailand book

Preparation:
Mix the blue powdered tempera with water until it resembles thin watercolor. Cover a table with newsprint and place the paint and brushes on top of it.

Directions:
1. Show pictures of Thailand and the people who live in Thailand from a resource book.
2. Explain that the children will be drawing pictures of the Thai Water Festival. Have the children brainstorm possible scenes to draw, for example, children playing in a puddle of water or people placing their pet fish in a river.
3. Give each child a sheet of white paper and assorted felt pens to draw Water Festival pictures.
4. When the pictures are drawn, demonstrate how to use very thin streaks of blue paint to coat the pictures.
5. When the pictures have dried, post them on a bulletin board labeled "The Water Festival in Thailand."

Literature Link:
• *Thailand* by Sylvia McNair (Children's Press, 1987).
This resource book has good color photographs to show children.

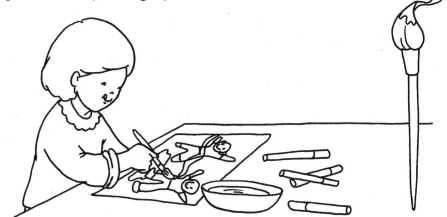

FESTIVAL OF LANTERNS

Materials:
Small paper bags (one per child), newspaper, confetti, yarn, scissors, tempera paint, paintbrushes

Preparation:
For each child, cut an arm-length strip of yarn. Place the paint, newspaper, confetti, yarn, scissors, and paintbrushes on a table.

Directions:
1. Explain that the Chinese Festival of Lanterns begins with the first full moon of the new year. Lanterns are decorated with glass beads and hung from homes.
2. Give each child a small paper bag. Have the children stuff their bags with crumpled sheets of newspaper.
3. Help children tie a piece of yarn around the tops of their bags to secure them.
4. Demonstrate how to gently push down on the "lanterns." This will give them a more traditional shape.
5. Children can paint the paper bag lanterns. To represent glass beads, the children can sprinkle confetti on the wet paint.
6. When the lanterns have dried, hang them from the classroom ceiling.

Option:
Sprinkle glitter on the lanterns when they are wet.

CLEAR/FUZZY

. . . .

Materials:
Clear/Fuzzy pictures (p. 194), reproduction of one of Monet's paintings (see Literature Links, below)

Preparation:
Duplicate and enlarge the Clear/Fuzzy pictures. Make one copy for each child.

Directions:
1. Tell the children about the painter named Claude Monet who painted a very famous series of pictures of water lilies. Show children a picture of one of these paintings.
2. Explain that some people think that Claude Monet painted the pictures in a "blurry" style because his eyesight was fading and he was simply painting what he saw.
3. Show children the Clear/Fuzzy pictures. Give each child a copy.
4. Have children color the fuzzy picture in each pair.

Optional:
Let children paint their own water lilies with watercolors.

Literature Links:
• *A Blue Butterfly: A Story About Claude Monet* by Bijou Le Tord (Doubleday, 1995).
• *Linnea in Monet's Garden* by Christina Bjork, drawings by Lina Anderson (Rabén & Sjögren, 1985).
This adorable book includes reproductions of Monet's work, as well as photographs of his home and garden at Giverny.

Clear/Fuzzy Pictures

DOTS, DOTS, DOTS

Materials:
Clear/Dotty Pictures (p. 196); "A Sunday Afternoon on the Island of La Grande Jatte" (New York Graphic Society), or another reproduction of one of Georges Seurat's works

Preparation:
Duplicate and enlarge the Clear/Dotty Pictures.

Directions:
1. Explain that a painter named Georges Seurat invented a style called pointillism. This word means that the pictures were actually a series of tiny dots of color. Show children a copy of one of Seurat's paintings.
2. Show children the dotty-picture side of the Clear/Dotty Pictures and have them try to guess what the dots represent.
3. Once all of the children have had a chance to guess, reveal the clear pictures.

Option:
Have children try out their own hands at pointillism. Provide markers or crayons and white paper and let children go dotty!

Literature Link:
• *The Painter's Eye: Learning to Look at Contemporary American Art* (Delacorte, 1991).
This book introduces ways of seeing, experiencing, and appreciating art.

©1997 Monday Morning Books, Inc.

Clear/Dotty Pictures

SPLISH, SPLASH

Materials:
Butcher paper, tempera paints, squeeze bottles, newsprint, smocks, reproduction of one of Jackson Pollock's works (see Literature Link, below)

Preparation:
Fill the squeeze bottles with tempera paint.

Directions:
1. Explain that a painter named Jackson Pollock was known for his "messy" style of art. He dripped and splashed paint on canvases. Show children a picture of Jackson Pollock's art.
2. Give children the opportunity to make their own splish/splash paintings. (Make sure to cover the work area with newsprint and the children's clothes with smocks. Or do this activity outside.)
3. Spread out butcher paper and provide children with squeeze bottles of paint to use to create their splish/splash pictures.
4. Post the completed pictures on a wall in the classroom.

Option:
Have children describe what their pictures make them think of. Write down their quotes and post them near the pictures.

Literature Link:
• *Jackson Pollock* by Elizabeth Frank (Abberville Press, 1983).

©1997 Monday Morning Books, Inc.

**Famous Artists
Science**

MOONLIGHT MAGIC

∙ ∙

Materials:
Full Moon pattern (p. 199), flashlight, tape, scissors, felt pen

Preparation:
Duplicate and enlarge the Full Moon pattern. Cut it out and tape it on
a wall.

Directions:
1. Explain that light comes from the sun and that it shines on Earth's
trees, mountains, lakes, people, and so on.
2. Explain that light allows us to see. Light is very important to painters.
It allows them to see colors, shadows, and shapes.
3. Point to the moon on the wall. Explain that the moon seems bright
at night because the sun shines on it. Without the sun, the moon would
not shine.
4. Turn off the lights in the classroom and shine the flashlight on the Full
Moon pattern. Explain that the flashlight is like the sun. Observe how
the moon is bright. It is reflecting the "sunlight."

Option:
Pass out paper, paint, and paintbrushes. Have the children paint a
picture in very dim light. Have the children observe whether it is more
or less difficult to see colors in dim light. Artists depend on light!

Literature Link:
• *Come Look with Me: Enjoying Art with Children* by Gladys S. Blizzard
(Thomasson-Grant, 1990).
This book presents 12 color reproductions of paintings, with
questions to stimulate discussions.

Full Moon Pattern

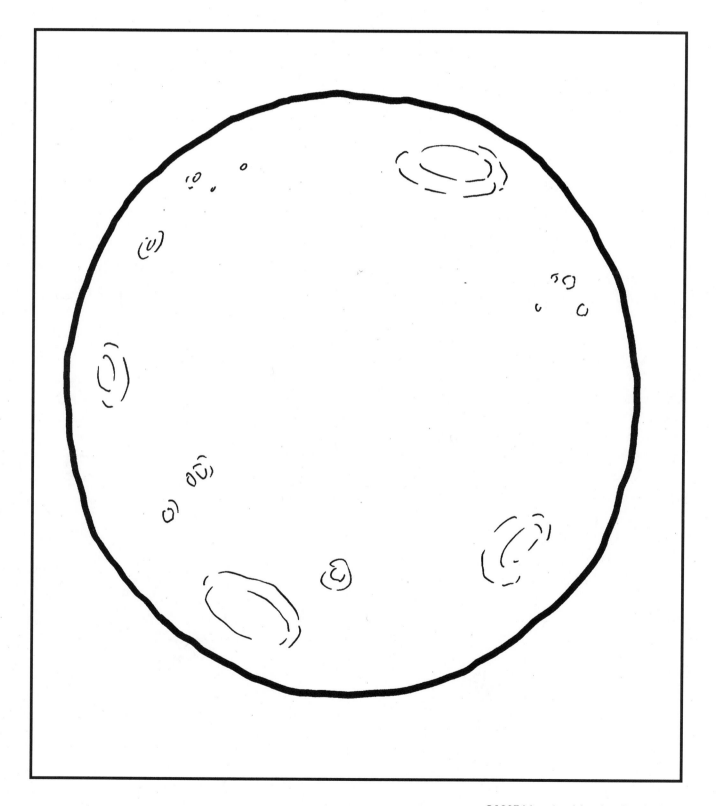

MIX-UPS

· ·

Materials:
Large white paper plates (one per child), paints in a variety of colors, paintbrushes with thin tips

Preparation:
Place the paints and paintbrushes on a table.

Directions:
1. Explain that a palette is a thin board with a thumb hole at one end. It is used by artists for holding and mixing paint colors.
2. Pass out the paper plates. These will be the children's palettes.
3. Have the children experiment with mixing colors. Encourage children to mix colors in small spaces in order to mix many batches on their paper plates.
4. Have the children try adding white and black to different colors. Also have them mix yellow and blue to make green, red and blue to make purple, yellow and red to make orange, black and white to make gray, and red and white to make pink.
5. Let the palettes dry. Display them on a wall.

Literature Link:
• *A Color of His Own* by Leo Lionni (Pantheon Books, 1975). A chameleon wishes that he didn't blend in with his surroundings. Luckily, he finds a friend to change colors with.

PAINTER'S MATH

· ·

Materials:
Palette patterns (p. 202), Painter Math Rhyme (pp. 203-204), scissors, crayons or markers, envelopes (one per child)

Preparation:
Duplicate a copy of the Palette patterns and Painter Math Rhyme for each child.

Directions:
1. Give each child a copy of the Palette patterns to color and cut out.
2. Read the Painter Math Rhyme to the children. Children can put the patterns in order as you recite the verses.
3. Let children store the Palette patterns and copies of the Painter Math Rhyme in envelopes to practice counting at home.

Literature Link:
• *Painting: Behind the Scenes* by Andrew Pekarik (Hyperion, 1992). This book discusses painting from an artist's point of view and shows how to discover the details in a painting.

Palette Patterns

Painter Math Rhyme (1-5)

A painter was mixing some paints on her tray.
She said, "I will start with one color today."
She dotted some yellow to color a sun.
She had only yellow, that's one color. (One)

A painter was mixing some paints on her tray.
She said, "I will add one more color today.
I have one dot of yellow, and now I'll add blue."
Instead of one dot of paint now there were . . . (two).

A painter was mixing some paints on her tray.
She said, "I will add one more color today.
I have yellow and blue, but I must paint a tree."
She mixed blue and yellow, got green,
    And had . . . (three)!

A painter was mixing some paints on her tray.
She said, "I will add one more color today."
She had blue, green, and yellow, but wanted one more.
So she added some red paint, and then she had . . . (four)!

A painter was mixing some paints on her tray.
She said, "I will add one more color today."
She wanted to paint a long, lonely drive.
She mixed up some gray paint,
    And then she had . . . (five).

Painter Math Rhyme (5-10)

A painter was mixing some paints on her tray.
She said, "I will add one more color today."
She wanted to paint some branches and sticks.
She mixed up some brown paint, and then she had . . . (six).

A painter was mixing some paints on her tray.
She said, "I will add one more color today."
She wanted to paint fluffy clouds in the heavens.
She added some white, and then she had . . . (seven).

A painter was mixing some paints on her tray.
She said, "I will add one more color today."
She was painting away, and it was getting late,
But she added some black, and then she had . . . (eight).

A painter was mixing some paints on her tray.
She said, "I will add one more color today."
She wanted another, and then she'd be fine.
She mixed up some orange, and then she had . . . (nine).

A painter was mixing some paints on her tray.
She said, "I will add one more color today.
This is my last color—I won't add one again."
She poured on some gold, and then she had . . . (ten).

Ten wonderful colors alive on her tray.
Ten shining, bright colors, she could paint with all day.
She'd paint a bright rainbow, an arc that would glow.
She'd paint a huge storm, with white sleet and snow.
She'd paint little children, just out having fun.
Then she'd wash up her tray, when she was all done.
In the morning, she'd start with a fresh brush and tray,
Who knew what great colors she'd mix the next day.

CUBISM

· ·

Materials:
Poster board, scissors, white construction paper, felt pens, crayons, reproduction of a picture done by one of the cubist artists (see Literature Link, below)

Preparation:
Cut the poster board into small squares. Make one square per child.

Directions:
1. Explain that a painter named Pablo Picasso developed a style of painting that he made famous. The style is called cubism and uses cube and square shapes. Show a picture by Picasso or one of the other cubist artists.
2. Pass out the poster board squares, white paper, felt pens, and crayons.
3. Demonstrate how to hold a square with one hand and trace its shape with a felt pen.
4. Encourage the children to make an interesting cube pattern on their papers, tracing as many cubes as they want. They can overlap them or trace them separately.
5. When the children are finished tracing, they can draw a picture over the cube shapes or color in the cubes.
6. Display the cube drawings on a bulletin board titled "Curious Cube Pictures."

Literature Link:
• *Pablo Picasso: Art for Children* by Ernest Raboff (Doubleday, 1968). This book is part of an amazing series that includes painters Marc Chagall, Paul Klee, Renoir, van Gogh, Michelangelo, Toulouse-Lautrec, Matisse, and more. Show children the pictures and read to them about the artists. For information, write to Harper & Row Junior Books, 10 East 53rd Street, New York, NY 10022.

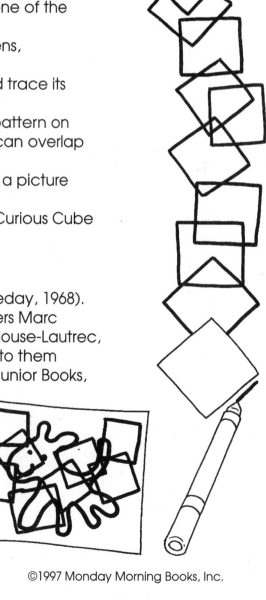

©1997 Monday Morning Books, Inc.

SWIRLY, SWIRLY NIGHT

. . . .

Materials:
Tempera paint in a variety of colors, paintbrushes, white construction paper, reproduction of van Gogh's "Starry, Starry Night" (see Literature Link, below)

Preparation:
Place the paints and paintbrushes on a table.

Directions:
1. Explain that Vincent van Gogh was a famous artist who often painted colorful and vivid pictures of things he saw outside. Show a reproduction of "Starry, Starry Night."
2. Give each child a sheet of paper. Explain that van Gogh painted with large swirling strokes. Some of the objects in his paintings, such as trees, stars, and flowers, look almost as though they are moving.
3. Have the children paint something using large, swirly strokes.
4. When the paintings have dried, have each child explain his or her painting to the class.
5. Display the paintings on a bulletin board titled "Inspired by van Gogh."

Literature Link:
• *A Weekend with van Gogh* by Rosabianca Skira-Venturi (Rizolli, 1993). This book includes reproductions of many of van Gogh's most famous works.

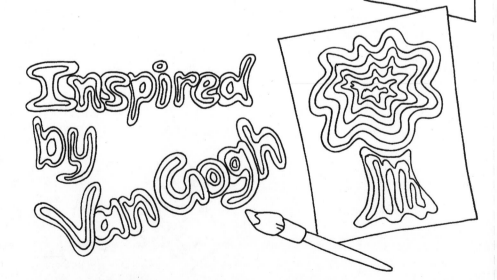

Chapter Six
Valentine's Day and Habitats

VALENTINE PARTNERS

. . . .

Materials:

White paper, scissors, map or globe, felt pen, box

Preparation:

Cut the white paper into small strips. Write one child's name on each strip. Place the strips in a box.

Directions:

1. Sit with the children in a circle. Explain that every holiday has a starting place. St. Valentine's Day is thought to have begun in Rome. Show Rome on a map or globe.
2. Pick two names from the box and read the names aloud. The two children picked can sit by each other.
3. Continue until every child has a Valentine partner.
4. Have the children think of kind messages to say to their friends.

Option:

Have the children make and exchange Valentine cards with their Valentine partners.

Literature Link:

• *Valentine's Day* by Joyce Kessel (Carolrhoda Books, 1981). Valentine's Day started more than 2,700 years ago! This nonfiction book includes this and many other interesting facts to share with your students.

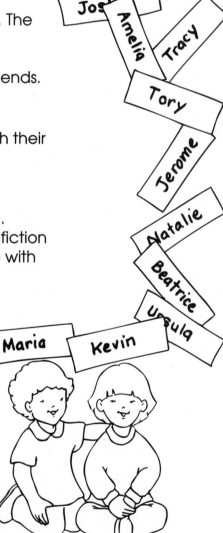

Valentine's Day
Phonics

POLLY PARROT

Materials:
Parrot pattern (p. 210), "P" Words (p. 211), scissors, crayons, glue

Preparation:
Duplicate a copy of the Parrot and "P" Words for each child.

Directions:
1. Have the children practice the sound of the letter "p" with you.
2. Introduce the Parrot pattern as Polly the parrot, and have the children repeat the rhyme with you.

> ## Polly the Parrot
> *Polly the parrot likes to play*
> *With Peter and Pamela*
> *On Valentine's Day.*
> *She likes to play and she likes to talk,*
> *But she only picks P words to squawk, squawk, squawk.*
> *Polly says, "Pool, and pig, and prop."*
> *Polly says, "Pat, and pink, and pop."*
> *Polly says, "Please, and pour, and pry."*
> *Polly says, "Let's eat Valentine's Day pie!"*

3. Pass out the Parrot and "P" Words. Have the children color in their parrots and cut out the words.
4. Sound out each "p" word with the children.
5. The children can glue their "p" words onto their Parrot patterns.
6. Post the finished parrot pictures on a "Polly Says" bulletin board.

Option:
Make a list of other "p" words with the children. Have them copy these words onto their "Polly the Parrot" posters.

Literature Link:
• *Polly Wants a Cracker*, a "Rookie Reader" by Bobbie Hamsa, illustrated by Jerry Warshaw (Children's Press, 1986).
What happens when Polly receives all the crackers she wants?

Parrot Pattern

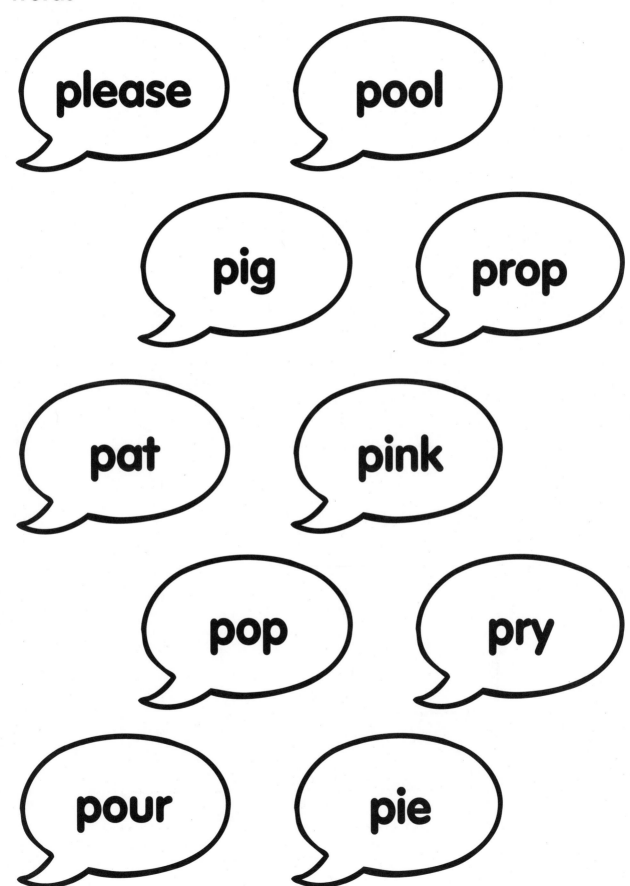

Pp Patterns

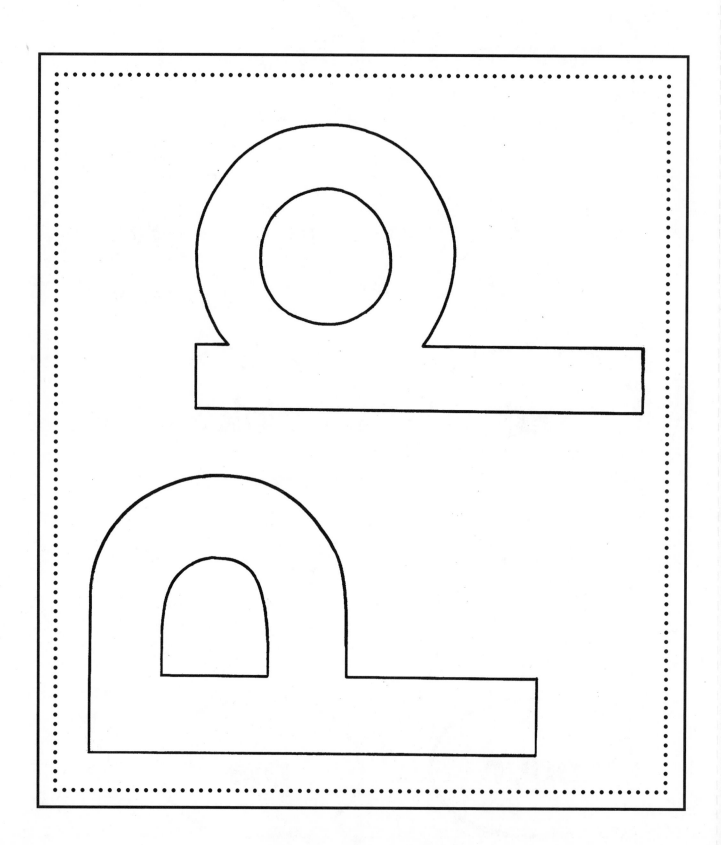

QUIZ SHOW

Materials:
Valentine's Questions (p. 214), "Q" Picture Cards (p. 215), pink paper, pen, scissors, box

Preparation:
Duplicate the Valentine's Questions onto pink paper and cut out. Place the questions in a box. Duplicate the "Q" Picture Cards and cut apart.

Directions:
1. Have the children repeat the "q" sound with you.
2. Show the box. Explain that it has questions inside it. Have the children repeat the word "questions."
3. Give each child a turn to answer a question. Give the children the clue that all of the answers have a "q" in them. If children don't know the answer, ask for volunteers. If no one can solve the question, hold up one of the picture clues or tell the answer and help children learn a new word and a definition. Put the question back in the box to ask again later.

Literature Link:
• *The Missing Tarts* by B. G. Hennessy (Viking, 1989).
When the Queen of Hearts discovers that her tarts have been stolen, she enlists the help of nursery rhyme characters.

Questions

- *If you were married to a king, what would you be? (queen)*

- *If someone tells you to "shh," they want you to be what? (quiet)*

- *If you are cold, you can wrap up in this type of blanket. (quilt)*

- *Sometimes feathers are called this. (quills)*

- *If you don't want to play a game anymore, you can do this. (quit)*

- *You can trade 25 pennies for this. (a quarter)*

- *If you want to play football, you can play this position. (quarterback)*

- *If you're a duck, you make this noise. (quack!)*

- *If your stomach is upset, you feel this way. (queasy)*

- *A type of bird with a plume on its head is this. (quail)*

- *You end a question with this. (question mark)*

- *Tests are sometimes called this. (quizzes)*

- *A fight is sometimes called this. (quarrel)*

- *A type of food with eggs and cheese is called this. (quiche)*

- *If you go very fast you are said to be this. (quick)*

- *If you step in this stuff, you sink! (quicksand)*

"Q" Picture Cards

Queen

A Duck Says... *Quack!*

Quick

Quicksand

Quiet

Quail

Queasy

A Quarrel *?@¿§#!!¿¿*

Quiz *QUIZ 1. 2. 3. 4. 5.*

Quiche

Quilt

I quit!

Question Mark

Quill

Quarter *LIBERTY 1987*

Quarterback

R IS FOR RED

. . . .

Materials:
Roses and Rubies pattern (p. 218), red crayons

Preparation:
Duplicate a copy of the Roses and Rubies pattern for each child.

Directions:
1. Say the letter "r" and have children repeat the sound with you.
2. Read the R Is for Red poem. Once you've read it, have children repeat it with you.

> ### R Is for Red
> *Roses are red,*
> *And rubies are, too.*
> *Red starts with /r/.*
> *And ruby does, too.*
> *Red hearts on valentines.*
> *Red hearts for you.*
> *R begins red,*
> *And rubies, too.*

3. Give each child a copy of the Roses and Rubies pattern to color with red crayons.
4. Post the finished pictures on a bulletin board called "Roses and Rubies." Post an enlarged copy of the poem nearby.

Literature Link:
• *The Encyclopedia of Gemstones and Minerals* by Martin Holden (Facts on File, 1991). This 303-page resource includes many illustrations of a wide variety of gems.

Roses and Rubies Pattern

Rr Patterns

ANIMAL VALENTINE

Materials:
Bowerbird pattern (p. 221), paper plates (one per child), green crayons, glue, scissors, small decorative items (twigs, confetti, flowers, pebbles, shells, leaves, marbles, feathers)

Preparation:
Duplicate a copy of the Bowerbird pattern for each child.

Bowerbird Facts:
• The bowerbird is found in New Guinea and Australia.
• A bowerbird will clear a space on the ground and cover it with small, colorful objects. These objects can be natural or man-made, such as pieces of glass or paper.
• Male bowerbirds build these displays to attract females.

Directions:
1. Describe the bowerbird and its attraction method to the children. This is the way this bird demonstrates affection.
2. Have the children each build a bowerbird display. Pass out the paper plates and green crayons. The children can color their plates green to represent cleared spaces, free from tall grass, twigs, and brush.
3. Pass out the glue and decorative items for the children to use to decorate their space.
4. Each child can show his or her finished plate and explain why it would attract a bowerbird.
5. Give the children copies of the Bowerbird pattern to color, cut out, and glue to their displays.

Literature Link:
• *Exotic Birds* by Marilyn Singer, illustrated by James Needham (Doubleday, 1990).
This large book includes many facts and pictures about interesting birds, including the bowerbird.

Bowerbird Pattern

VALENTINE'S MATH

Materials:
Valentine Math patterns (p. 223), Valentine Math Rhyme (pp. 224-225), scissors, crayons, envelopes (one per child)

Preparation:
Duplicate a copy of the Valentine Math patterns and Valentine Math Rhyme for each child.

Directions:
1. Give each child a copy of the Valentine Math patterns to color and cut out.
2. Read the Valentine Math Rhyme to the children.
3. Have the children manipulate the patterns while the rhyme is read aloud.
4. Children can store the patterns and rhymes in envelopes for additional at-home practice.

Option:
Substitute names of children in your class for the names of the children in the Math Rhyme who give valentines to Jennifer.

Literature Link:
• *Valentine Friends* by Ann Schweninger (Scholastic, 1988). Bunnies tell this charming Valentine's Day story as they prepare for the big celebration.

Valentine Math Patterns

Valentine Math Rhyme (1-5)

On Valentine's Day, when Jennifer counted,
She found that her valentines hadn't amounted
To what she'd expected. And why was that so?
She'd given ten valentines away, you know.
She thought that she'd get ten valentines back.
Instead, she got none, not even from Jack.

No valentines received on Valentine's Day.
What a sad feeling, what a bad day!
But Valentine's Day had only begun.
Anne gave her a heart, and now Jen had . . . (one).

And then Jason said, "Here, I've got one for you."
Now Jen had another, and that one made . . . (two).

Two valentines—wow!—Jen smiled with glee!
Then Jack gave her one, and then she had . . . (three).

Three valentines—cool—she could not ask for more,
But Kate gave her one, and then she had . . . (four).

Four valentine cards. The day came alive.
And when Ben gave her one, the total hit . . . (five).

Valentine Math Rhyme (5-10)

Five Valentine hearts. What a colorful mix.
Then James gave her one, and then she had . . . (six).

Six cards for Jen. Then Kim gave one more.
She had . . . (seven) cards. What a great score!

Seven cards for Jennifer. Wasn't that great?
Emily gave her another, and then she had . . . (eight).

Eight cards were amazing. Eight cards were fine.
But Beth gave her one, and then she had . . . (nine).

Nine beautiful cards! Nine cards for Jen.
The teacher gave her one, and then she had . . . (ten).

On Valentine's Day, Jennifer's smile shined.
Ten of her friends had given her valentines.
She was happy and joyful, she smiled and beamed,
Then counted her cards with the lacy white seams.

One, two, three, four, five, all pretty for Jen.
Six, seven, eight, nine, and one more made ten.
Ten valentine cards, on Valentine's Day.
Jenny counted them all, then shouted, "HOORAY!"

225

Valentine Number Sets

♡	1	♡♡	2
♡♡♡	3	♡♡♡♡	4
♡♡♡♡♡	5	♡♡♡♡♡♡	6
♡♡♡♡♡♡♡	7	♡♡♡♡♡♡♡♡	8
♡♡♡♡♡♡♡♡♡	9	♡♡♡♡♡♡♡♡♡♡	10

LOVE HEARTS

. . . .

Materials:
Poster board, scissors, felt pens, glue, white paper

Preparation:
Cut out a large heart shape from poster board. Trace the heart's outline onto a large sheet of white construction paper. Trace a heart for each child.

Directions:
1. Ask for volunteers to share something they love: a person, animal, book, thing, act of doing something, and so on.
2. Explain that the children will be making Love Hearts. Pass out the heart outlines and felt pens. Have the children draw the things that they love inside the hearts.
3. During group time, ask for volunteers to share what they have drawn inside their hearts.

Literature Link:
• *My First Valentine's Day Book* by Marian Bennett (Children's Press, 1985).
This easy-to-read nonfiction book tells about making Valentine's Day cards, having parties, and sending cards to friends.

NEON VALENTINES

· ·

Materials:
Small sheets of white construction paper, crayons (red, pink, and black), paper clips (one per child)

Preparation:
None

Directions:
1. Give each child a sheet of white construction paper to color using the red and pink crayons. Have the children press hard so the colors are bold. Each sheet should be colored entirely.
2. When the papers are colored pink and red, have the children color each sheet entirely with black crayon. None of the pink or red should show.
3. Give each child a paper clip to bend open. Using one end of the paper clip, the children should make small scratches on the black-colored papers. The colors beneath will be revealed. They will appear bright with a neon shine.
4. Children can draw hearts or designs with the paper clips. They can make many pictures on the papers.

Option:
Mount the finished pictures on red or pink construction paper. Or fold them in half for children to use as Valentine's Day cards.

Literature Link:
• *Things to Make and Do for Valentine's Day* by Tomie de Paola (Franklin Watts, 1976).
This colorfully illustrated book of Valentine's Day projects includes games that children can play with their friends.

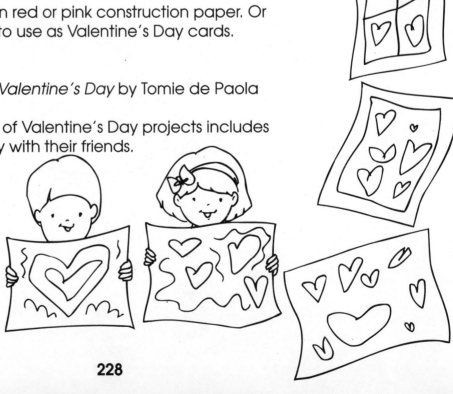

DESERT LIFE

· ·

Materials:
Desert Animal and Plant patterns (p. 230), scissors, butcher paper, white paper, felt pens, tape

Preparation:
Draw a large cactus (see the pattern on p. 230) on a sheet of butcher paper and tape it on a wall. Duplicate a copy of the Desert Animal patterns for each child.

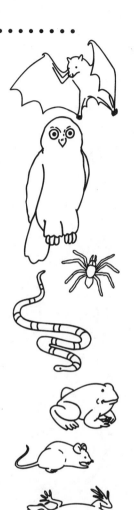

Desert Facts:
• It is hot during the day, but it can get cold at night.
• There is little water.
• Plants that live in the desert have no leaves.
• Some plants have thorns.
• Some plants blossom in the night if it rains.

Directions:
1. Explain that a habitat is the kind of place where a person, animal, or plant lives. The desert is a habitat for lizards, snakes, cacti, and so on.
2. Describe a desert and give each child a copy of the Desert Animal patterns to color and cut out.
3. When the children have finished coloring their pictures, they can tape the animal pictures around the butcher paper cactus.

Option:
Have the children use green tempera paint to color the cactus.

Literature Link:
• *Desert Life* by Barbara Taylor, photographs by Frank Greenaway (Dorling Kindersley, 1992).
These four-color photos make the desert come to life!

Desert Animal and Plant Patterns

SLUSH MAKER

Materials:
A few large ice cubes, clear drinking glass, three tablespoons of salt, books about ponds (see "Literature Links," below)

Preparation:
Make sure the glass is clean and dry.

Directions:
1. Explain that when the air becomes very cold, pond water can freeze. Ice forms a layer over the water.
2. Show children a picture of a pond. Discuss different animals that live in ponds.
3. Place the ice cubes and salt into the clean glass.
4. Have the children watch the glass very closely.
5. The outside of the glass should become wet. This is because the coldness in the glass turns the moisture in the air into water.
6. Have the children continue to watch the glass. The ice cubes eventually turn to slush.
7. Explain to the children that there is moisture or water in the air around us. When the air becomes cold, the water can form into rain, snow, or ice. When the air becomes warmer, the ice melts.

Literature Links:
• *Pond and River* by Steve Parker (Random House, 1988).
This photo essay explores the range of plants and animals found in and near ponds.
• *Trip Day* by Harriet Ziefert, illustrated by Richard Brown (Little, Brown, 1987).
Mr. Rose's class takes a field trip to find out about pond life.

CROCODILE EYES

• •

Materials:
Crocodile Counting pattern (p. 233), pencils

Preparation:
Duplicate a copy of the Crocodile Counting pattern for each child.

Crocodile Facts:
• Crocodiles can be found in swamps in the United States.
• Some crocodiles live in parts of Africa, India, and South America.
• Crocodiles live near water.
• Crocodiles can swim with only their eyes and nostrils out of the water.

Directions:
1. Describe the crocodile's habitat.
2. Read the last fact in the box. Ask the children what advantage this might give the crocodile.
3. Say The Crocodile Chant. Clap to establish a rhythm.

> ### The Crocodile Chant
> *Do the crocodile count and do it right,*
> *For the crocodile chomps with all his might.*
> *When swimming in the river in the heat of the day,*
> *Don't miss that crocodile coming your way!*

4. Pass out the Crocodile Counting patterns and have the children count the number of crocodiles. (A pair of eyes equals one crocodile.)
5. Have the children circle the correct number of crocodiles at the top of the page. Then have them compare answers.

Literature Link:
• *Amazing Crocodiles and Reptiles* by Mary Ling, photographs by Jerry Young (Knopf, 1991).
This Eyewitness Book includes photographs and text depicting the habits, diets, and characteristics of several kinds of crocodiles.

Crocodile Counting Pattern

10 12 15 18

COUNTING CROCODILES

• •

Materials:
Crocodile patterns (p. 235), Crocodile Math Rhyme (pp. 236-237), blue construction paper, crayons, scissors, envelopes (one per child)

Preparation:
Duplicate a copy of the Crocodile patterns and the Crocodile Math Rhyme for each child.

Directions:
1. Give each child a copy of the Crocodile patterns to color and cut out.
2. Give each child a sheet of blue construction paper to use for a stream.
3. Have the children place their crocodiles on the blue construction paper.
4. Read the math rhyme to the children. As you read the rhyme, the children can move their crocodile patterns out of the "stream."
5. Let the children take home their crocodiles and a copy of the Crocodile Math Rhyme in the envelopes. Children can continue their counting practice at home.

Literature Link:
• *Lyle, Lyle Crocodile* by Bernard Waber (Houghton Mifflin, 1965). Lyle is perfectly happy living with the Primms on E. 88th until Mr. Grumps next door changes all that!

Three little crocodiles swimming in a stream.
You can see their eyes and they're looking mean.
One little crocodile basks in the sun, ...

Crocodile Patterns

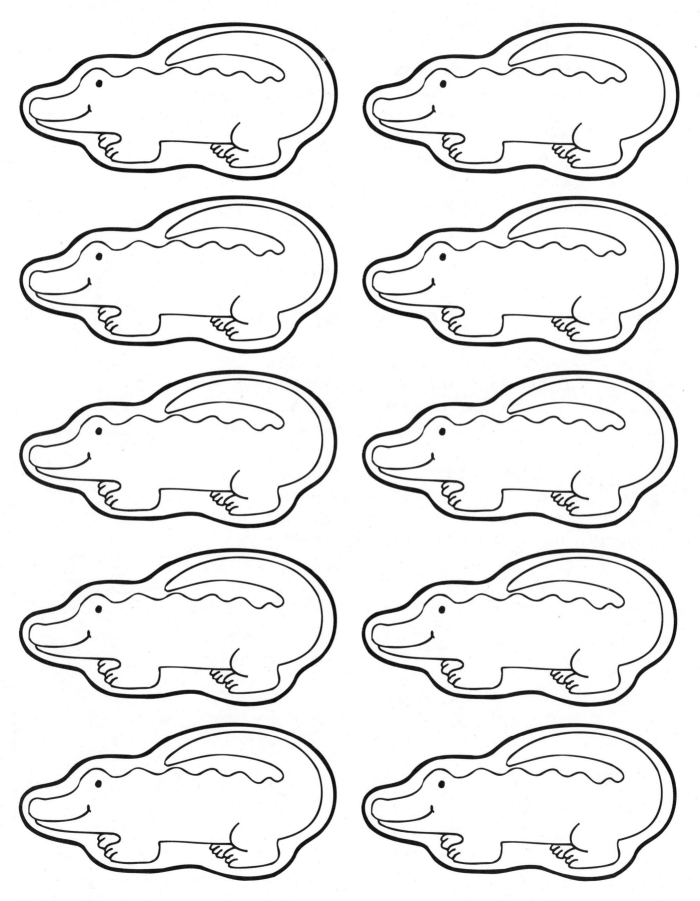

Crocodile Math Rhyme (10-5)

Ten little crocodiles swimming in the stream.
You can see their eyes and they're looking mean.
One little crocodile swims off to dine,
And when that croc goes away, that leaves . . . (nine).

Nine little crocodiles swimming in the stream.
You can see their eyes and they're looking mean.
One little crocodile swims off on a date,
And when that croc goes away, that leaves . . . (eight).

Eight little crocodiles swimming in the stream.
You can see their eyes and they're looking mean.
One little crocodile decides to swim away.
Now there are . . . (seven) crocodiles left to play.

Seven little crocodiles swimming in the stream.
You can see their eyes and they're looking mean.
One little crocodile goes off to play some tricks,
And when that croc goes away, that leaves . . . (six).

Six little crocodiles swimming in the stream.
You can see their eyes and they're looking mean.
One little crocodile decides she's had enough.
Now there are . . . (five) crocodiles looking tough.

Crocodile Math Rhyme (5-0)

Five little crocodiles swimming in the stream.
You can see their eyes and they're looking mean.
One little crocodile crawls onto shore,
And when that croc goes away, that leaves . . . (four).

Four little crocodiles swimming in the stream.
You can see their eyes and they're looking mean.
One little crocodile rests under a tree,
And when that croc goes away, that leaves . . . (three).

Three little crocodiles swimming in the stream.
You can see their eyes and they're looking mean.
One little crocodile has something to do,
And when that croc goes away, that leaves . . . (two).

Two little crocodiles swimming in the stream.
You can see their eyes and they're looking mean.
One little crocodile basks in the sun,
And when that croc goes away, that leaves . . . (one).

One little crocodile swimming in the stream.
You can see his eyes and he's looking mean.
Being all alone just isn't any fun,
And when that croc goes away, that leaves . . . (none).

No little crocodiles looking mean.
Now it's safe to swim in the cool, fresh stream.
All the other animals come out to play.
It's a lot of fun when the crocs are away.

237

Crocodile Number Sets

🐊	1	🐊🐊	2
🐊🐊	3	🐊🐊🐊🐊	4
🐊🐊🐊🐊🐊	5	🐊🐊🐊🐊🐊🐊	6
🐊🐊🐊🐊🐊🐊🐊	7	🐊🐊🐊🐊🐊🐊🐊🐊	8
🐊🐊🐊🐊🐊🐊🐊🐊🐊	9	🐊🐊🐊🐊🐊🐊🐊🐊🐊🐊	10

238

'ROUND THE CLOCK RHINO

Materials:
"'Round the Clock Rhino" Rhyme (p. 240), Clock pattern (p. 241), brads (one per child), crayons or markers, scissors, hole punch

Preparation:
Duplicate a copy of the Clock pattern for each child.

Rhinoceros Facts:
- The rhinoceros' habitats are grasslands.
- Grasslands are areas with a great amount of grass.
- The rhino is a grazer. This means it eats all day long.

Directions:
1. Give each child a copy of the Clock pattern to color.
2. Have the children color and cut out the long and short hands of the clock. Discuss the concept that the long hand of a clock points to the minutes and the short hand points to the hours. Show children how this works on a clock in your classroom.
3. Punch a hole in the center of each clock and help the children attach the hands to their clock faces using brads.
4. Teach the children the 'Round the Clock Rhino Rhyme.
5. As you say the chant, have children move the arms of their clocks to the appropriate times. Start the clocks at eight.

Literature Link:
- *Rainbow Rhino* by Peter Sis (Knopf, 1987).
Rhino's good friends are lured away from him by promises of adventure. In the end, his friends discover that true friendship is worth more than any adventure.

'Round the Clock Rhino Rhyme

The rhino eats at eight o'clock,
And walks and walks and walks.

At nine o'clock he munches more,
Chewing on the grassland floor.

He eats again at ten o'clock.
And walks and walks and walks and walks.

At eleven o'clock he chews and chews—
This rhino needs some walking shoes!

He eats again at twelve o'clock,
And walks and walks and walks.

At one and two, he chews and chews,
This rhino has no time to talk!

At three and four and five and six,
He walks and walks and walks and walks.

At seven, eight, and nine o'clock,
He chews a little and rests a lot.

By ten o'clock he sleeps at last,
And what do you think he dreams of?
GRASS!

Clock Pattern

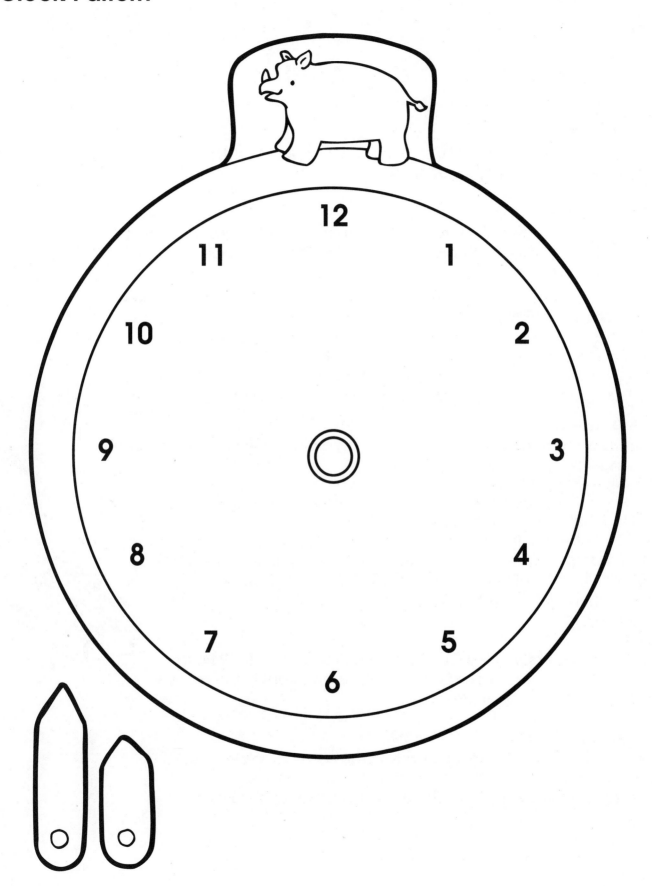

GO APE!

Materials:
Orangutan pattern (p. 243), glue, orange tempera paint, paintbrushes, yarn (red, brown, or orange), scissors

Preparation:
Duplicate a copy of the Orangutan pattern for each child. Cut yarn into short pieces. Make a handful for each child. Place the glue, paint, paintbrushes, and yarn on a table.

Orangutan Facts:
• Orangutans have large eyes, two large nostrils, and puffy cheeks.
• They have long orange hair all over their faces.
• Orangutans live in the hot, jungle-like forests of Sumatra and Borneo.

Directions:
1. Explain that the children will be making a paint and yarn picture of an orangutan.
2. Give each child an Orangutan pattern.
3. Have the children use the orange paint to cover the entire picture, avoiding painting the eyes and nose.
4. Once the paint dries, have the children glue strings of yarn all over the orangutans' faces. They should avoid covering the eyes and nose.
5. Post the completed pictures on a bulletin board labeled "Orangutan Faces in the Forest."

Option:
Duplicate a copy of the Orangutan Habitat pattern (p. 244) for each child. Have the children color the orangutans in the picture orange and the forest green.

Literature Link:
• *Among the Orangutans* by Evelyn Gallardo (Chronicle, 1993). This nonfiction book offers an insightful look at the lives of orangutans in a rain forest. The book has fantastic pictures!

Orangutan Pattern

Orangutan Habitat Pattern

Chapter Seven
St. Patrick's Day and Amphibians

St. Patrick's Day
Circle Time

CLOVER WISHES

∙ ∙

Materials:
Clover pattern (p. 247), globe, green crayons, scissors, pen

Preparation:
Duplicate a copy of the Clover pattern for each child.

Ireland Facts (and Two Myths):
- Ireland is sometimes called "The Emerald Island" because its landscape is green.
- Shamrocks, which are a type of clover, grow all over Ireland.
- According to legend, wearing a shamrock is the only way to frustrate a leprechaun that's teasing you.
- Shamrock means three-leaved.
- Everyone's Irish on March 17, St. Patrick's Day!

Directions:
1. Have children help you find Ireland on the globe.
2. Explain that finding a four-leaf clover is rare and considered to bring good luck.
3. Give each child a Clover pattern to cut out.
4. Have the children make wishes on their clovers and help them write their wishes on their clovers.
5. Have the children decorate their clovers using green crayons.
6. Post the clovers on a bulletin board labeled "I Love Ireland!"

Option:
Provide green glitter or sequins for children to use to further decorate their clovers.

Literature Link:
- *Daniel O'Rourke* retold by Gerald McDermott (Viking, 1986). In this classic Irish tale, Daniel O'Rourke dances, eats, and drinks too much at a party. His dreams that night reflect his overindulgences.

Clover Pattern

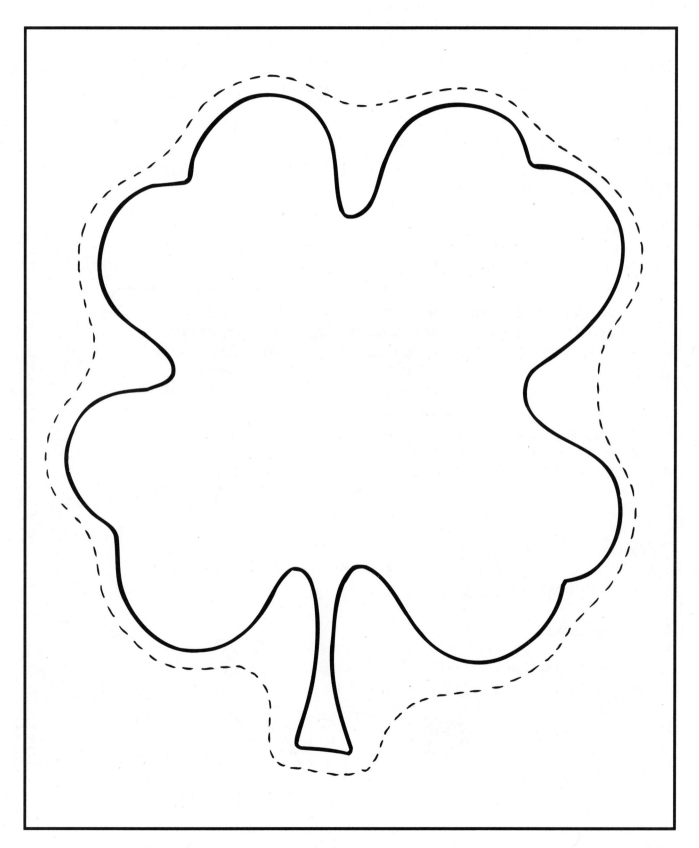

"S" STORYTELLING

. . . .

Materials:
Story patterns (p. 249), crayons or markers, scissors, felt scraps, glue, felt board

Preparation:
Duplicate the Story patterns, color, and cut out. Attach a small piece of felt to the back of each card.

Directions:
1. Practice the sound of the letter "s" with the children.
2. Read the following "Starts with S" story.

> **Sometime** last **September**, a **small** leprechaun named **Sam stashed** his gold inside a **slipper**. The **slipper** was **soft** and **specked** with **silver**. **Sam slid** the **slipper** into a **secret** place. Then **Sam** heard a **sound!** It was **Sam's** friend, **Silly Sarah**. **Sarah saw** the **slipper** and **snatched** it. Then **Silly Sarah slipped** on **Sam's slipper**. Wasn't **Sarah silly**?

3. Read the story again slowly and have the children raise their hands whenever you read a word that starts with "s."
4. As you read the story, put the Story patterns on the felt board.
5. Let children take turns retelling the story using the felt board and Story patterns.

Option:
Ask for a volunteer storyteller. This child will stand before the class and make up a story involving "s" sounds.

Literature Link:
• *Tim O'Tool and the Wee Folk*
by Gerald McDermott
(Viking, 1990).
A poor man named
Tim comes upon a group
of partying leprechauns
who change his luck forever.

Sometime last September, a small leprechaun named Sam stashed his gold inside a slipper. The slipper was soft and...

Story Patterns

RIDING THE "T" TRAIN

Materials:
Train patterns (p. 252), "T" Picture patterns (p. 253), crayons or markers, scissors, hole punch, brads or short pieces of yarn

Preparation:
Duplicate a copy of the Train patterns and a copy of the "T" Picture patterns for each child.

Directions:
1. Give each child a copy of the Train patterns to color and cut out.
2. Have the children imagine that they are riding on a train and looking out the windows.
3. Repeat the rhyme a few times for the children.

> ### The "T" Train Rhyme
> *We're riding a train through Ireland,*
> *And what do you think we see?*
> *Trucks and towers and telephone poles,*
> *All things that start with T.*

4. Give each child a copy of the "T" Picture patterns to color and cut out.
5. Have the children glue one picture pattern to each train car.
6. Children can punch a hole in each train car and attach them using brads or pieces of yarn.
7. Post the trains in rows on a bulletin board labeled "Take the T Train."

Literature Link:
• *St. Patrick and the Peddler* by Margaret Hodges (Orchard, 1993). The beauty of the Irish countryside is evident in this tale of a young boy, a peddler, and St. Patrick, who appears in a dream.

Train Patterns

Tt Patterns

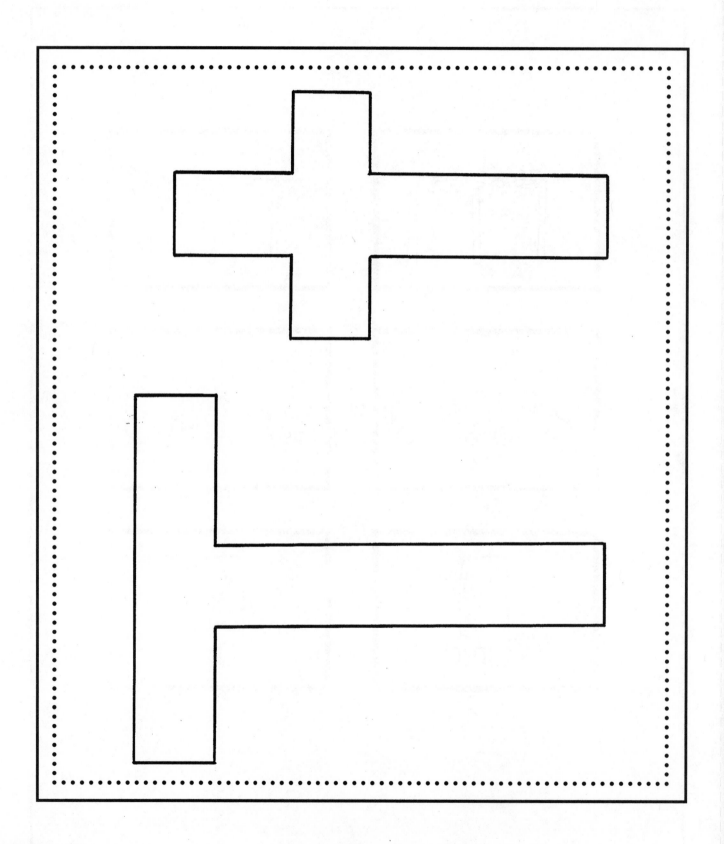

UNPACKING A SUITCASE

Materials:
Suitcase pattern (p. 256), "U" pictures, scissors, glue, crayons

Preparation:
Duplicate a copy of the Suitcase pattern and "U" pictures for each child.

Directions:
1. Have the children practice the sounds of the letter "u." They can repeat words with the long "u" sound, such as, "unicorn," "unicycle," "unique," and "Utah"; and words with the short "u" sound, such as, "unpack," "uncle," "under," and "up."
2. Give each child a copy of the Suitcase pattern and "U" pictures to color and cut out.
3. Repeat the Unpacking Rhyme with the students until they have learned it.

> **Unpacking Rhyme**
> *I unpacked my suitcase in Ireland.*
> *I had brought all my favorite toys:*
> *A stuffed unicorn, a unique unicycle,*
> *And a ukulele to make lots of noise!*

4. Have the students glue the "U" pictures onto their suitcases.
5. Post the completed suitcase pictures on a "We're Going to Ireland" bulletin board.

Literature Link:
• *Mary McLean and the St. Patrick's Day Parade* by Steven Kroll (Scholastic, 1991).
This is a beautifully illustrated tale about life in Ireland in the 1850s. The McLean family must leave their hut and set sail for America.

Suitcase Pattern

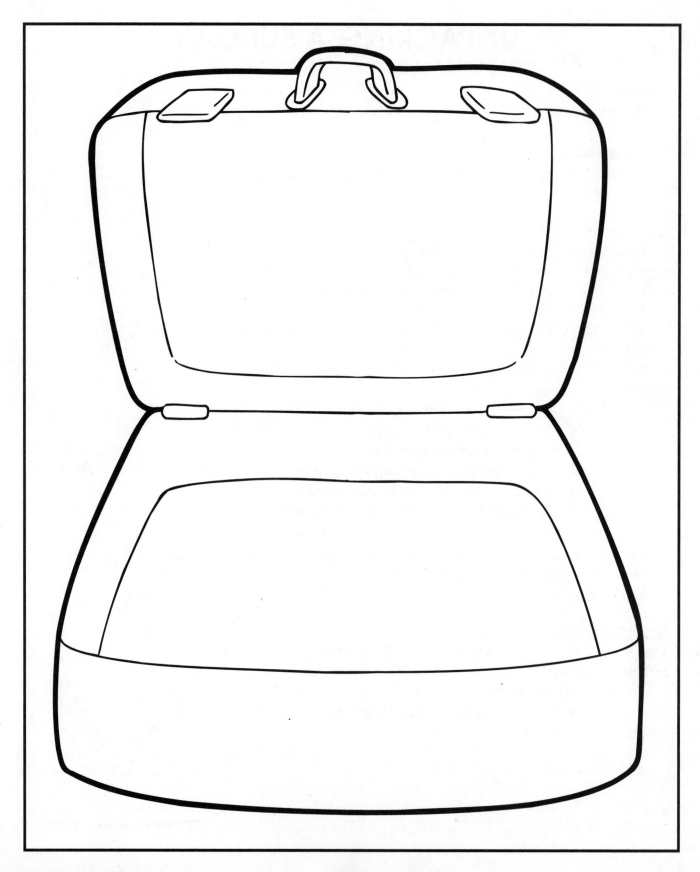

"U" Pictures

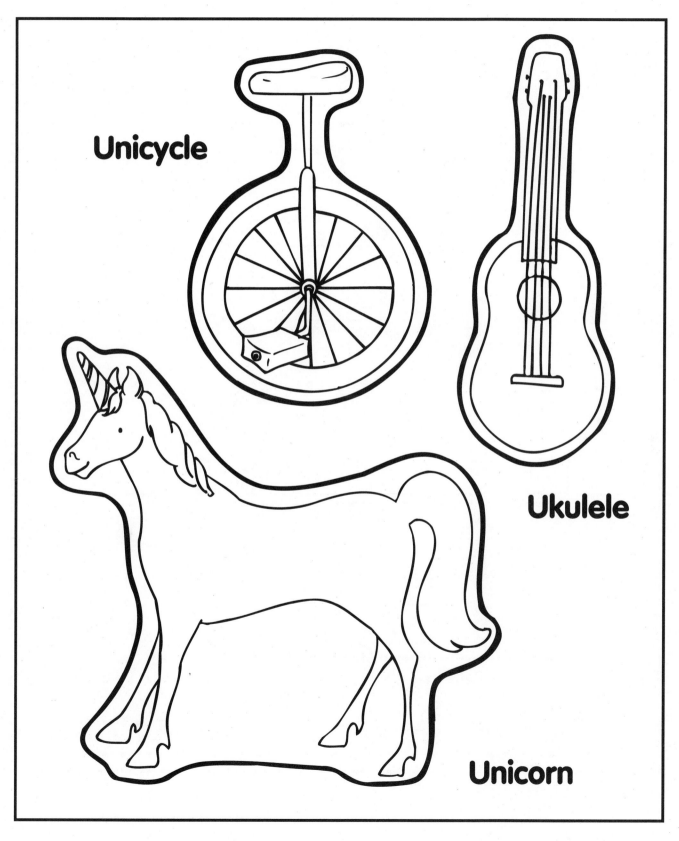

Unicycle

Ukulele

Unicorn

Uu Patterns

LEPRECHAUN TRICK 1

. . . .

Materials:
Penny, glass, lemon juice

Preparation:
None.

Directions:
1. Tell the children that a leprechaun might do the following trick to turn dirty pennies shiny again.
2. Place a darkened penny in a glass.
3. Pour lemon juice into the glass until the penny is covered.
4. Let the penny sit in the lemon juice for at least 15 minutes.
5. Remove the penny from the glass and rinse it off. (It should be shiny and clean.)
6. Explain that pennies are made of copper. New pennies are bright and shiny. Over time, pennies become dirty and the copper turns dark. Lemon juice is an acid and this acid cleans the pennies.

Literature Link:
• *The Irish Piper* by Jim Latimer, illustrated by John O'Brien (Scribner's, 1991).
This read-to story tells the tale of the Pied Piper, who lives in the west of Ireland.

©1997 Monday Morning Books, Inc.

LEPRECHAUN TRICK 2

· ·

Materials:
Sheet of construction paper, tape, book

Preparation:
None.

Directions:
1. Have the children imagine that a leprechaun told them he would give them a pot of gold if they could support a book on a sheet of paper.
2. Hold a sheet of paper so an edge of the paper is touching a table. Let go. The children will see that the paper cannot stand on its own.
3. Have the children brainstorm ways the paper could support the book.
4. Roll the paper into a tube and tape the edges together.
5. Stand the tube of paper on an end and place a book on top of it. The tube of paper will support the book!
6. Explain to the children that a tube or column shape is very strong. This shape is used to hold up buildings.

Option:
Slowly add more books to the top of the tube. Have the children observe how many books the tube will support.

Literature Link:
• *The Legend of Knockmany* (Scholastic, 1993).
In this Big Book multicultural tale, one giant is afraid to fight another.

LEPRECHAUN GOLD

Materials:
Gold patterns (p. 262), Leprechaun Math Rhyme (pp. 263-264), yellow crayons or markers, scissors, envelopes (one per child)

Preparation:
Duplicate a copy of the Gold patterns and the Leprechaun Math Rhyme for each child.

Directions:
1. Give each child a copy of the Gold patterns to color and cut out.
2. Read the Leprechaun Math Rhyme to the children.
3. The children can manipulate the Gold patterns to help them answer the problems.
4. Place the Leprechaun Math Rhyme and the Gold patterns in envelopes to send home with the children. The children can continue to practice counting with their families.

Option:
Point out the ordinal numbers in the rhyme: first, second, third, fourth, fifth. Use the Leprechaun Ordinal patterns (p. 265) to help illustrate this concept. Children can place the patterns in the correct order according to the ordinal numbers and the rhyme.

Literature Link:
• *Clever Tom and the Leprechaun* (Scholastic, 1988). All Tom has to do to get the leprechaun's gold is catch him. But this isn't as easy as it sounds!

©1997 Monday Morning Books, Inc.

Gold Patterns

Leprechaun Math Rhyme (1-3)

In Ireland, I was told,
If you find a leprechaun, he'll give you gold.
So I searched the hillsides under the sun,
And found myself a leprechaun.
This first little man was dressed all in green,
With a bright green top hat and a suit like a bean.
He said, "Well, I guess you've had your fun."
And he gave me a gold coin. Then I had . . . (one).

In Ireland, I was told,
If you find a leprechaun, he'll give you gold.
So I searched the hillsides under the sun,
And I found myself a leprechaun.
This second man was dressed like a king,
With a jade green crown and an emerald ring.
He said, "Well, there's nothing I can do,
Except give you a coin." And then I had . . . (two).

In Ireland, I was told,
If you find a leprechaun, he'll give you gold.
So I searched the hillsides under the sun,
And I found myself a leprechaun.
This third little fellow was taking a nap.
He had green clothes on and a bright green cap.
I woke him up and he looked at me.
He gave me a coin. And then I had . . . (three).

Leprechaun Math Rhyme (3-5)

In Ireland, I was told,
If you find a leprechaun, he'll give you gold.
So I searched the hillsides under the sun,
And I found myself a leprechaun.
This fourth little fellow was dressed in a suit,
With a satin bow tie and a pair of green boots.
He said, "Well, I know you must want one more.
I will give you a coin." And then I had . . . (four).

In Ireland, I was told,
If you find a leprechaun, he'll give you gold.
So I searched the hillsides under the sun,
And I found myself a leprechaun.
This fifth fine fellow sat under a tree,
And he didn't seem angry when he saw me.
Instead, he said, "Well, sakes alive!"
And he gave me a coin. And then I had . . . (five).

I had five gold coins that jangled in tune.
I had five gold coins, as bright as the moon!
I said my thanks to my leprechaun friends,
And now, everyone, my tale's come to an end!

Leprechaun Ordinal Patterns

GREEN THINGS

. . . .

Materials:

Green tissue paper scraps, green construction paper, green glitter, green tempera paint, paintbrushes, glue, green felt pens, newsprint, chalk, tape

Preparation:

Cover a table with newsprint. Place the paint, paintbrushes, tissue paper scraps, construction paper, felt pens, and glitter on the table.

Directions:

1. Have the children make green pictures using the assorted art materials.
2. When the pictures have dried, tape them on a bulletin board labeled "Green Things."

Option:

Duplicate the Clover pattern (p. 247) onto green construction paper and cut the patterns out to use as a border around the bulletin board.

Literature Link:

• *St. Patrick's Day in the Morning* by Eve Bunting (Ticknor and Fields, 1980).
A young boy wants to be in the St. Patrick's Day parade, but everyone thinks he's too young.

WOVEN GOLD

Materials:
Green construction paper, yellow or gold construction paper, glue, felt pen, scissors

Preparation:
Make a green construction paper "loom" for each child by cutting seven to nine slits in each sheet of construction paper (as shown). Cut the yellow or gold construction paper into strips. (Cut about 10 strips for each child.)

Directions:
1. Tell the children that they will each be making a leprechaun's gold place mat!
2. Demonstrate how to weave the gold strips in and out of the green place mats.
3. When the gold strips are woven in, children can glue down the ends of the strips.
4. Have the children turn the mats over and glue down any additional loose ends.
5. Have the children sit with the place mats on the rug. Ask each child the question, "If you were a leprechaun, and ate only green and yellow food, what would you eat off your place mat?"

Option:
Have children use large sheets of green construction paper and larger gold strips to make giant place mats.

Literature Link:
• *Jamie O'Rourke and the Big Potato* by Tomie de Paola (G. P. Putnam's Sons, 1992). In this Irish tale, a lazy farmer grows the biggest potato ever seen.

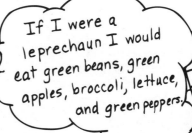

If I were a leprechaun I would eat green beans, green apples, broccoli, lettuce, and green peppers.

HALF-AND-HALF

. . . .

Materials:
Animal patterns (p. 269), Environment pattern (p. 270), crayons or colored markers, large sheet of construction paper, pen, scissors

Preparation:
Duplicate the Animal patterns, color, and cut out. Duplicate and enlarge the Environment pattern and color it.

Directions:
1. Display the Environment pattern and point out to the children the two types of environments shown: land and water.
2. Explain that some animals live on land and others live in the water. Post a fish picture in the water and a deer picture on the land.
3. Explain that there is a very special kind of animal that lives in water part of its life and on land the rest of its life. Explain that this type of animal is called an amphibian.
4. Discuss the four main types of amphibians and post their pictures on the Environment pattern. These animals are: frogs, toads, salamanders, and newts.

Option:
Duplicate the Animal and Environment patterns for the children to take home.

Animal Patterns

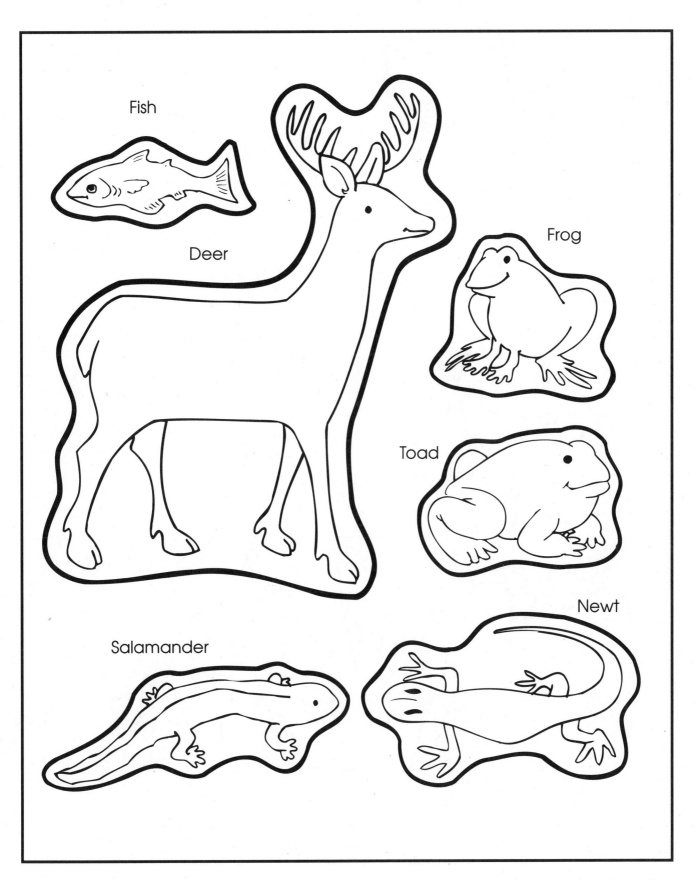

Fish

Deer

Frog

Toad

Newt

Salamander

Environment Pattern

EGG TO FROG

Materials:
Egg to Frog patterns (p. 272), crayons, scissors, white envelopes (one per child)

Preparation:
Duplicate a copy of the Egg to Frog patterns for each child.

Directions:
1. Explain the process through which a tadpole turns into a frog.

> **First, a mother frog lays hundreds of eggs in water.**
> **Second, a tadpole hatches out of each egg.**
> **Third, the tadpole grows bigger and bigger.**
> **Fourth, the tadpole grows back legs.**
> **Fifth, the tadpole grows front legs.**
> **Sixth, the tadpole becomes a frog!**

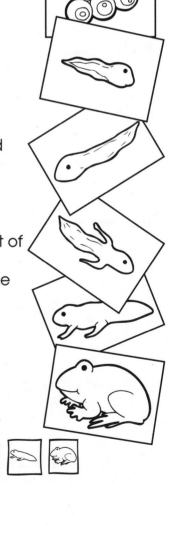

2. Give each child a copy of the Egg to Frog patterns to color and cut out.
3. Repeat the six steps as the children place their pictures in order from left to right.
4. When the children's pictures are in order, ask for a volunteer to explain the steps. This child can bring his or her pictures to the front of the class and explain each one.
5. Children can store their Egg to Frog patterns in envelopes or take them home to share with their families.

Option:
Attach a piece of felt to the back of each pattern. Describe the stages of a tadpole's life by placing the patterns in order on a flannel board.

Egg to Frog Patterns

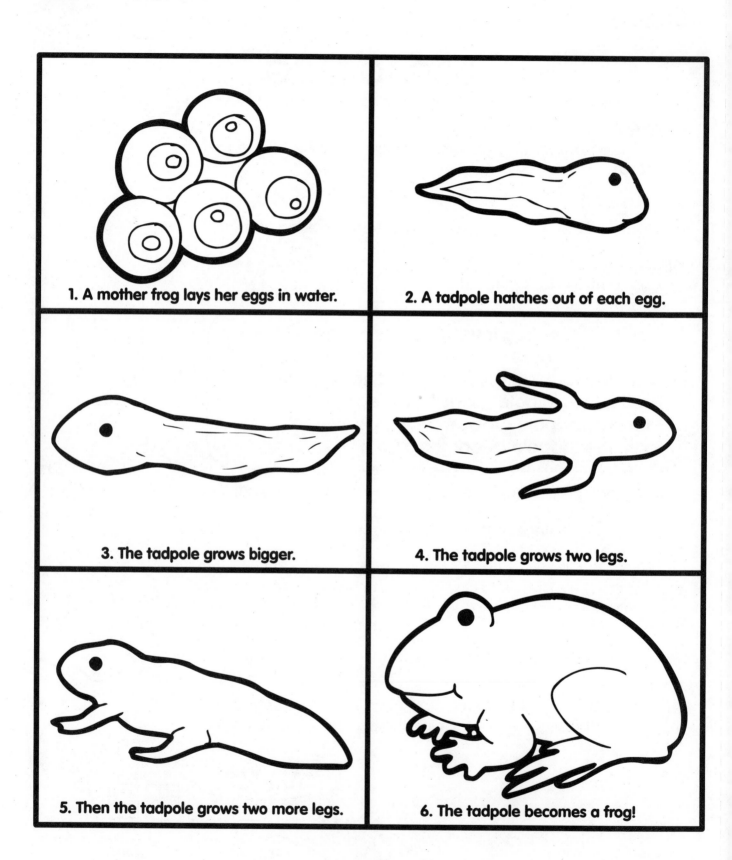

1. A mother frog lays her eggs in water.

2. A tadpole hatches out of each egg.

3. The tadpole grows bigger.

4. The tadpole grows two legs.

5. Then the tadpole grows two more legs.

6. The tadpole becomes a frog!

TADPOLE MATH

• •

Materials:
Tadpole Action Verses (pp. 274-275), Tadpole patterns (p. 276), Lake pattern (p. 277), scissors, crayons or markers, stapler, paper plates (1 1/2 per child), glue

Preparation:
Duplicate a copy of the Tadpole and Lake patterns and the Tadpole Action Verses for each child.

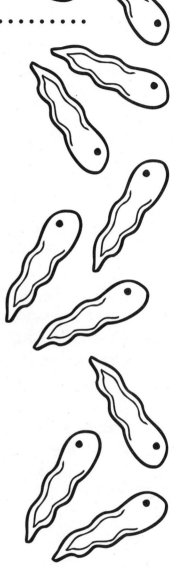

Directions:
1. Give each child a copy of the Tadpole and Lake patterns to color and cut out.
2. Give each child 1 1/2 paper plates. Demonstrate how to staple the half plate onto the full plate to make a pocket.
3. Children can glue the lake patterns onto the front of the pockets.
4. Have the children place all of their tadpoles in the lake pockets.
5. Read the Tadpole Action Verses. Have the children figure out the number of tadpoles left in each verse by taking their tadpoles out of the "water."
6. Place the Tadpole Patterns and Tadpole Action Verses in the lake pockets to send home with the children. The children can continue to practice counting with their families.

Option:
Have the children act out the Tadpole Action Verses. When you read the first line of each verse, have the children hold up their fingers to indicate how many tadpoles are in the lake. When you read the second line of each verse, children can use their arms to "dip" and "dive," and they can "give their tails a shake." At the third line, when one tadpole becomes a frog, children can jump like frogs. For the final line, children can hold up their fingers to indicate how many tadpoles are left in the lake. For the very last verse, children can "ribbit" and "croak."

Tadpole Action Verses (10-5)

Ten little tadpoles swimming in the lake,
They dip and dive and give their tails a shake.
One little tadpole turns into a frog.
Now there are . . . (nine) tadpoles in the bog.

Nine little tadpoles swimming in the lake,
They dip and dive and give their tails a shake.
One little tadpole turns into a frog.
Now there are . . . (eight) tadpoles in the bog.

Eight little tadpoles swimming in the lake,
They dip and dive and give their tails a shake.
One little tadpole turns into a frog.
Now there are . . . (seven) tadpoles in the bog.

Seven little tadpoles swimming in the lake,
They dip and dive and give their tails a shake.
One little tadpole turns into a frog.
Now there are . . . (six) tadpoles in the bog.

Six little tadpoles swimming in the lake,
They dip and dive and give their tails a shake.
One little tadpole turns into a frog.
Now there are . . . (five) tadpoles in the bog.

Tadpole Action Verses (5-0)

Five little tadpoles swimming in the lake,
They dip and dive and give their tails a shake.
One little tadpole turns into a frog.
Now there are . . . (four) tadpoles in the bog.

Four little tadpoles swimming in the lake,
They dip and dive and give their tails a shake.
One little tadpole turns into a frog.
Now there are . . . (three) tadpoles in the bog.

Three little tadpoles swimming in the lake,
They dip and dive and give their tails a shake.
One little tadpole turns into a frog.
Now there are . . . (two) tadpoles in the bog.

Two little tadpoles swimming in the lake,
They dip and dive and give their tails a shake.
One little tadpole turns into a frog.
Now there is . . . (one) tadpole in the bog.

One little tadpole swimming in the lake,
He dips and dives and give his tail a shake.
This little tadpole turns into a frog.
Now there are . . . (no) tadpoles in the bog.

No little tadpoles swimming in the lake.
They all are frogs, now, for goodness sake!
You can hear them singing as they sit on dry land.
They "croak" and they "ribbit" in their froggy band!

Tadpole Patterns

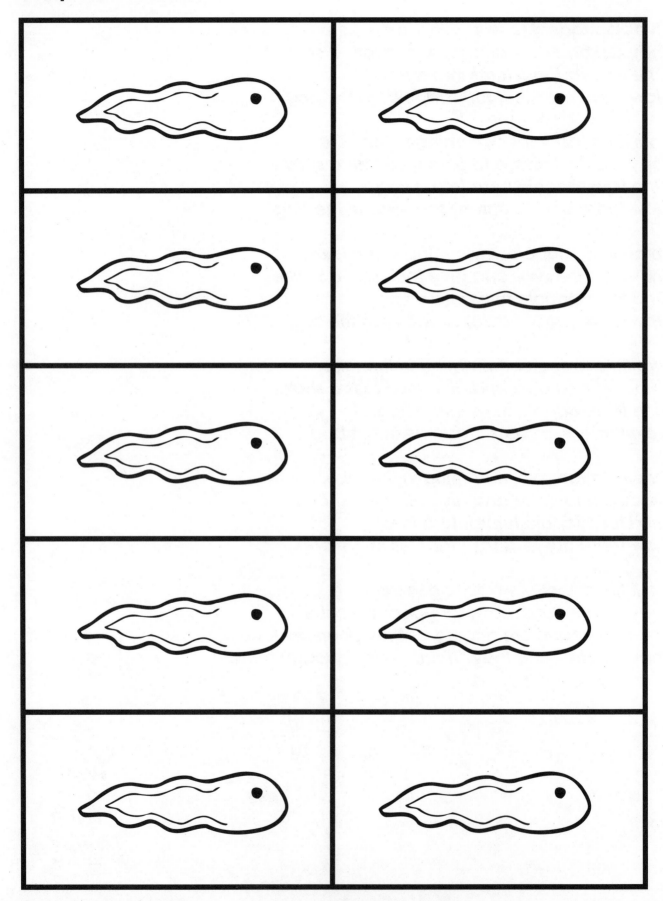

Lake Pattern

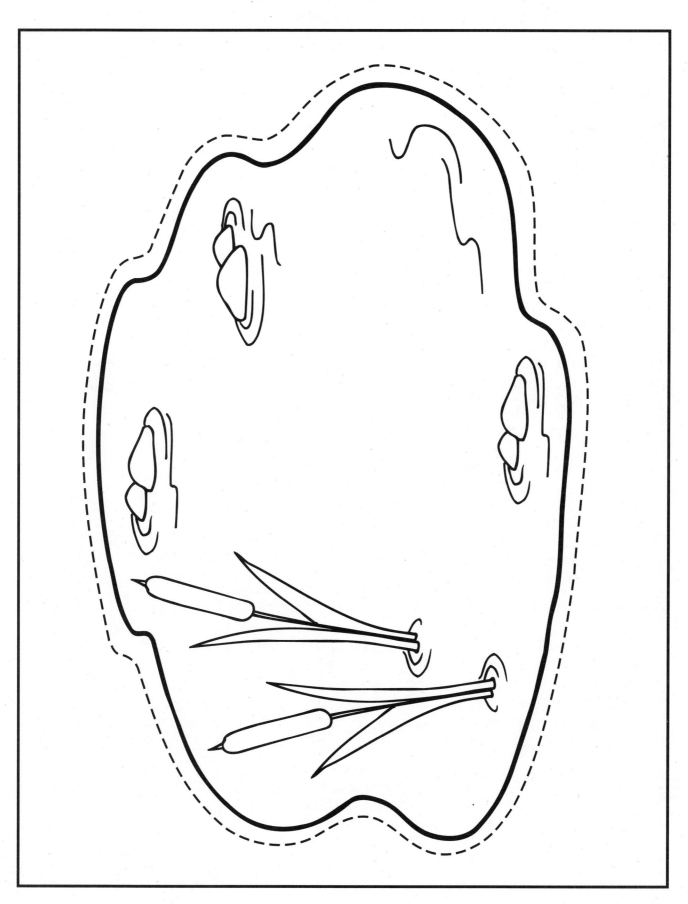

LILY PAD FROGS

Materials:
Frog patterns (p. 279), Lily Pad pattern (p. 280), blue construction paper, scissors, crayons

Preparation:
Duplicate a copy of the Frog and Lily Pad patterns for each child.

Directions:
1. Give each child a copy of the Frog and Lily Pad patterns to color and cut out. They don't have to cut out the Mama frog sitting on the lily pad.
2. Give each child a sheet of blue construction paper to serve as the frog pond. Children can place their lily pad on the blue paper and their frogs on the lily pad.
3. Teach the children the Mama Frog Chant.

Mama Frog Chant
Mama frog, mama frog,
Sat on a log,
Teaching her babies to swim.
"Jump into the water,
And swim like an otter,
Jump, Number Ten, jump in!"

4. Have each child jump one frog off the lily pad and onto the blue paper.
5. Repeat the chant, changing the number each time. Children will jump another frog into the pond after each verse.
6. Continue until the number one frog has jumped into the pond.
7. When you reach the ending verse, children can jump their frogs back onto their lily pads. Begin with the number one frog and end with number ten.

Mama frog, mama frog,
Sat on a log,
And saw that her babies had gone.
Come here, come here,
Number One, froggy dear,
You're swimming way too long!

Frog Patterns

Lily Pad Pattern

MUD PUPPY POPS

. . . .

Materials:
Mud Puppy patterns (p. 282), brown paper, scissors, brown and white tempera paint, paintbrushes, Popsicle sticks (one per child), small paper cups (one per child), newsprint

Preparation:
Cut a small slit at the bottom of each paper cup so a Popsicle stick can be pushed through. Place the paper cups, Popsicle sticks, paint, and paintbrushes on a newsprint-covered table. Duplicate the Mud Puppy patterns onto a sheet of brown paper and cut out.

. . . .
Mud Puppy Facts:
- Mud puppies are large salamanders that live in the mud.
- Mud puppies can be found near ponds or streams.
- Mud puppies hunt for food by quickly springing out of the mud to catch insects. They hunt early in the morning or in the evening.
. . . .

Directions:
1. Place the Mud Puppy patterns on brown paper for the children to observe. Explain that mud puppies blend in with their surroundings.
2. Have the children paint the Popsicle sticks brown. Once the paint dries, they can add white eyes with the white tempera paint.
3. Have the children paint the cups brown. These will represent the holes that mud puppies spring from to catch food.
4. Once the cups are dry, the children can push the mud puppies up through the slits in the paper cups.
5. Have the children sit together with their mud puppies.
6. Teach the children The Mud Puppy Poem. Have the children begin with their mud puppies hiding in the mud.

> ### The Mud Puppy Poem
> *Mud puppy hiding in the soft, brown mud,*
> *Get ready, get set, for some insect grub!*

7. Have the children remain quiet so that they don't scare the insects. Choose a child to say "Pop!" When this child says "Pop!" the children can pop up their mud puppies. Give each child a turn.

Mud Puppy Patterns

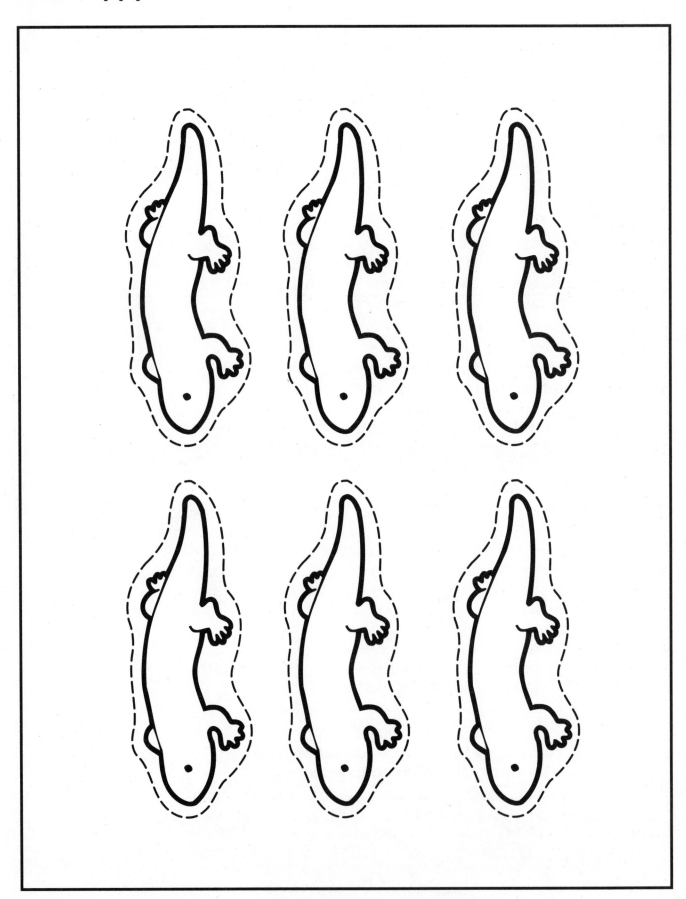

Chapter Eight
Spring and Farm Animals

NAME THAT BABY

. . . .

Materials:
Baby Animal Chant (p. 285), Animal Puppets (pp. 286-290), crayons or markers, scissors, Popsicle sticks, glue, envelopes (one per child)

Preparation:
Duplicate a copy of the Baby Animal Chant and the Animal Puppets for each child.

Directions:
1. Explain that many animals have babies in the spring. Some spring babies have different names than their parents.
2. Give each child a copy of the Animal Puppets to color and cut out.
3. Have the children glue one Popsicle stick to the back of each puppet and let the puppets dry.
4. Have the children hold up the appropriate puppets while you read the chant.
5. Let the children take their puppets and copies of the chants home to share with their families.

Option:
Duplicate the Animal Puppet patterns, color, cut them out, and laminate (if desired). Let the children try to match the babies with the parents.

Literature Link:
• *Animal Babies* by Harry McNaught (Random House, 1977). This easy-to-read book describes 20 baby animals, including a foal, a fawn, and a joey.

Baby Animal Chant

A baby dog is called a puppy.
A cow is called a calf.
A skunk is called a kitten—
Now, isn't that a laugh?

A baby swan is called a cygnet.
A deer is called a fawn.
Have you ever seen a joey
Jump across the lawn?

A baby shark is called a cub.
A bear is called one, too.
A goat is called a kid—
And, hey, so are you!

A baby cat is called a kitten.
An owl is an owlet.
A frog is called a tadpole,
And an eagle is an eaglet.

Baby birds are called nestlings,
But partridges are cheepers.
Tigers are called whelps,
And mackerels are tinkers.

A baby duck is called a duckling.
A horse is called a colt.
A pig is called a suckling,
And a zebra is a foal.

A baby rabbit is a bunny.
A goose is called a gosling.
A pigeon is a squeaker,
And a cod is called a codling.

But what about the joey?
Well, I'll give you a clue.
It lives inside the pouch
Of a mama kangaroo!

285

Animal Puppets

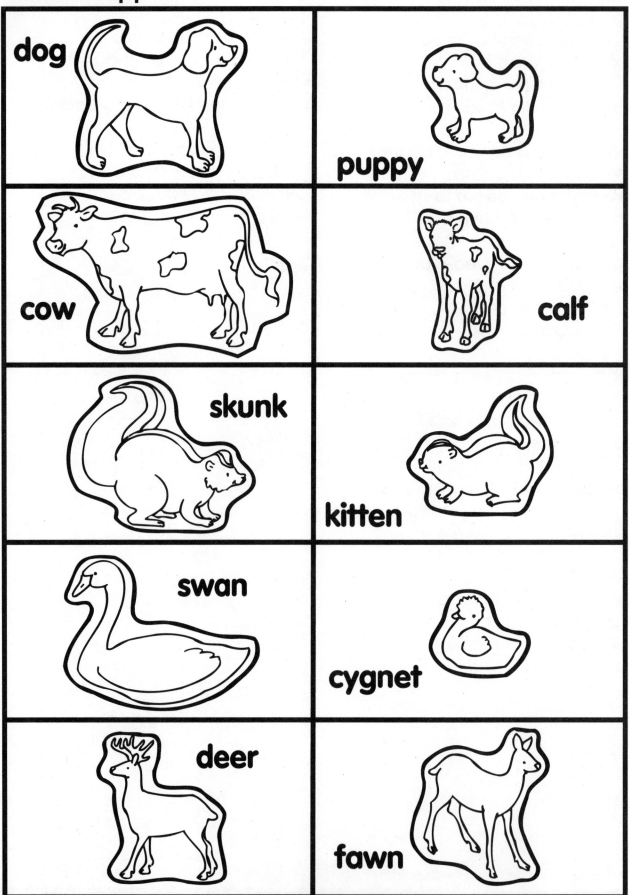

dog

puppy

cow

calf

skunk

kitten

swan

cygnet

deer

fawn

Animal Puppets

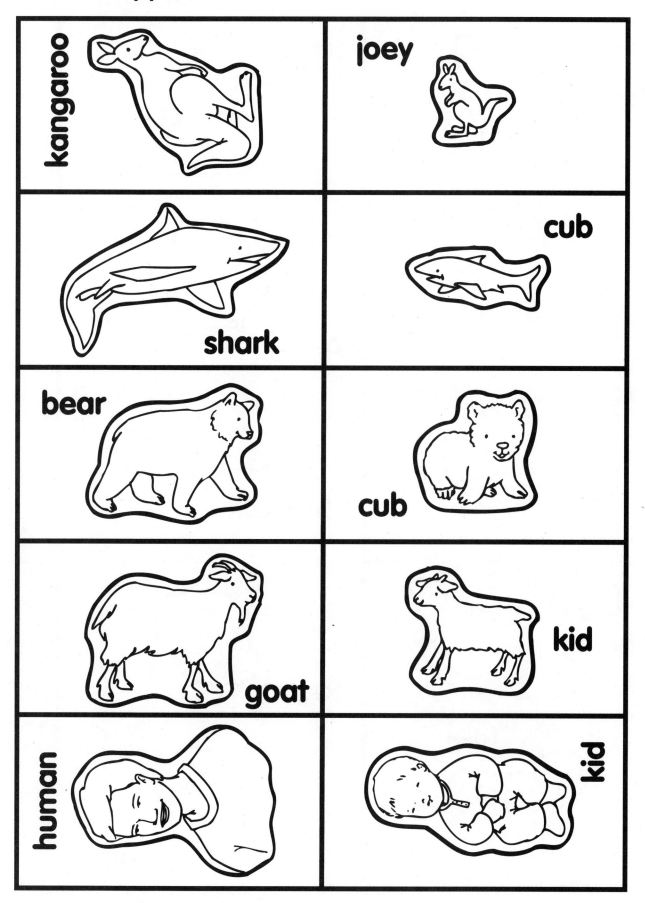

kangaroo

joey

shark

cub

bear

cub

goat

kid

human

kid

Animal Puppets

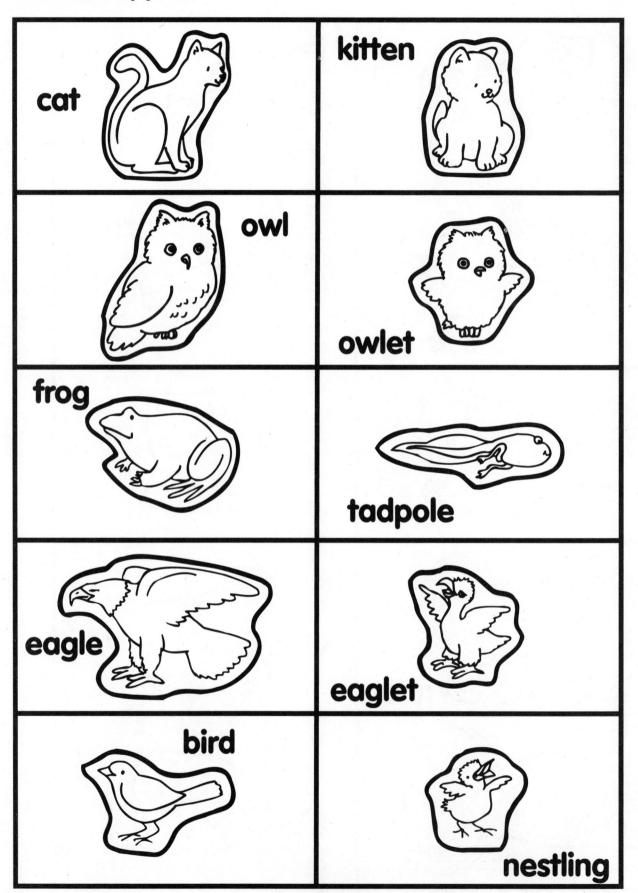

cat

kitten

owl

owlet

frog

tadpole

eagle

eaglet

bird

nestling

Animal Puppets

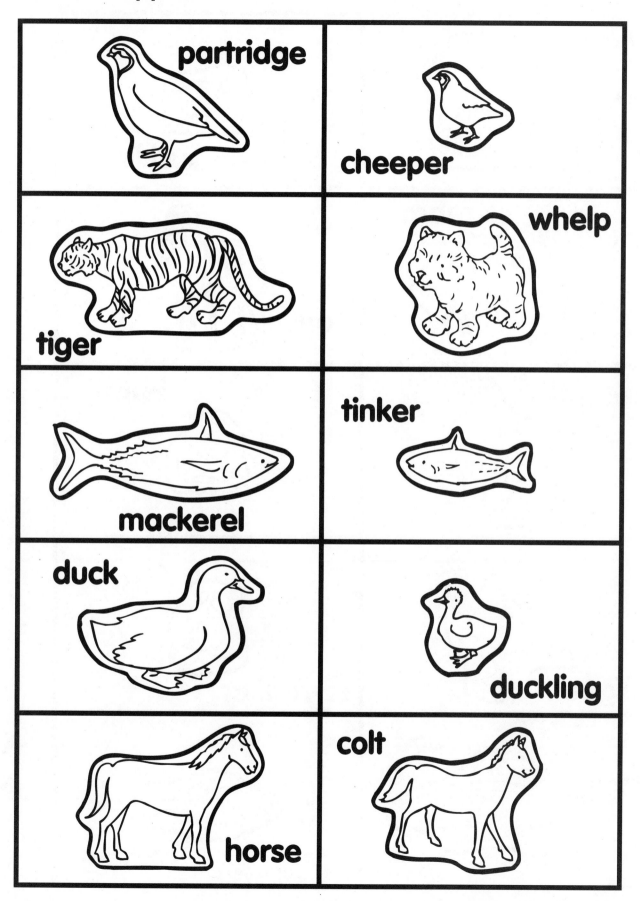

partridge

cheeper

whelp

tiger

tinker

mackerel

duck

duckling

colt

horse

Animal Puppets

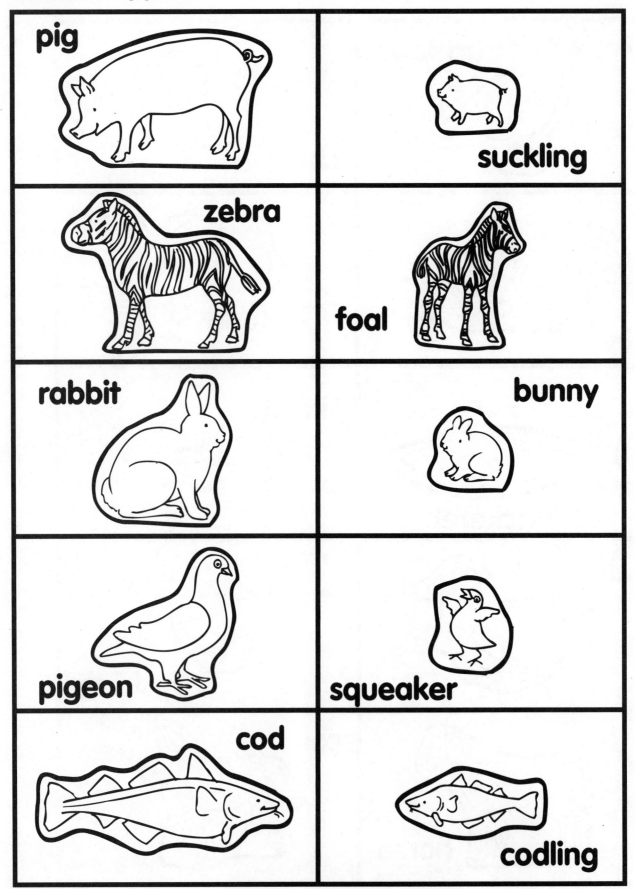

pig

suckling

zebra

foal

rabbit

bunny

pigeon

squeaker

cod

codling

VAN GOGH'S VASE

Materials:
Vase pattern (p. 292), crayons, colored chalk, scissors, glue, colored construction paper, print of van Gogh's "Sunflowers" (if available)

Preparation:
Duplicate a copy of the Vase pattern for each child.

Directions:
1. Have the children repeat the sound of the letter "v" with you.
2. Remind the children of the painter Vincent van Gogh. (Children can practice saying the painter's name, which has two v's.) If possible, show a picture of van Gogh's "Sunflowers." Explain that the children will be making pictures of spring flowers in vases.
3. Give each child a copy of the Vase pattern to color and cut out.
4. Children can glue their vases to colored construction paper backgrounds.
5. Provide colored chalk for children to use to draw flowers blooming from their vases. In the center of each flower, children can draw the letter v.

Literature Link:
• *Vincent van Gogh: Art for Children* by Ernest Raboff (Doubleday, 1968).
Show children the pictures by van Gogh and read to them about the artist. For information, write to Harper & Row Junior Books, 10 East 53rd Street, New York, NY 10022.

Vase Pattern

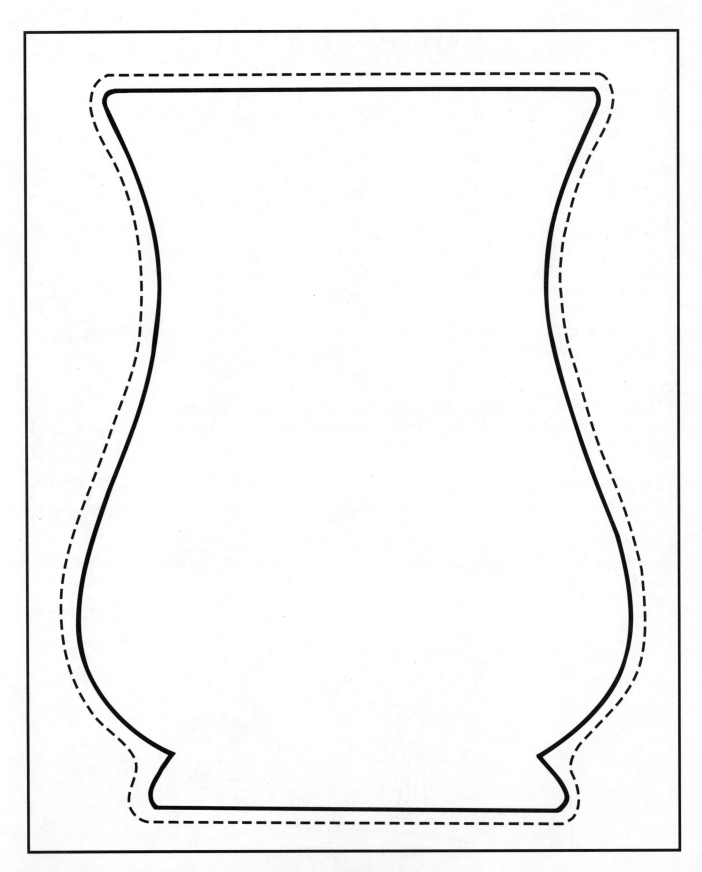

Vv Patterns

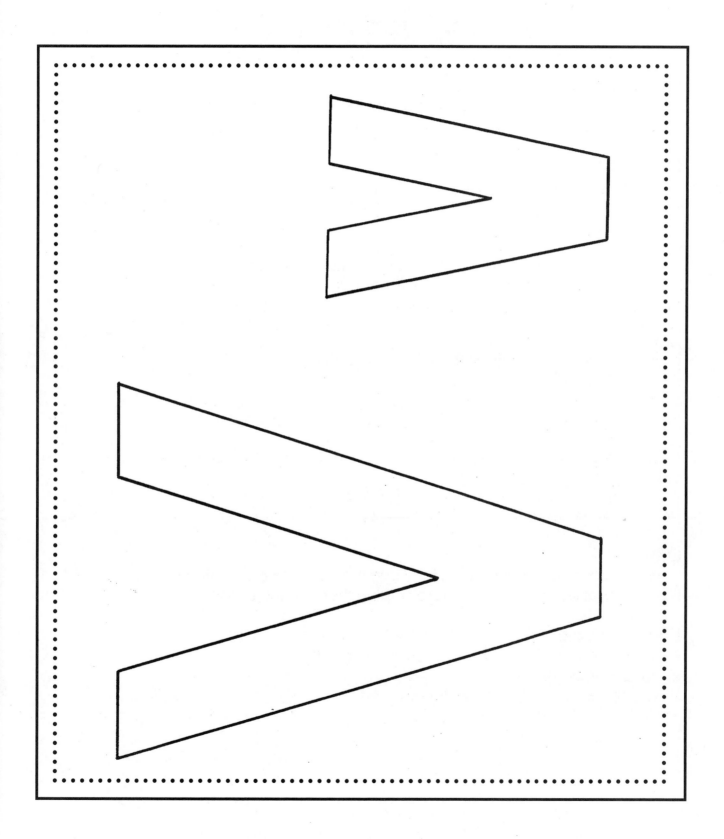

WATER LILIES

Materials:
Water Lily patterns (p. 295), butcher paper, crayons, tempera paint, paintbrushes, scissors, glue

Preparation:
Duplicate a copy of the Water Lily patterns for each child. Cut a large sheet of butcher paper for children to use to make a mural.

Directions:
1. Have the children repeat the sound of the letter "w" with you.
2. Remind the children of the painter Monet and his famous masterpiece, "Water Lilies." If possible, show a picture of this painting.
3. Explain that the children will be working together to make their own water lily mural.
4. Give each child a copy of the Water Lily patterns to color with crayons and cut out.
5. Have the children work together to paint a watery background on the butcher paper. They can copy the colors used by Monet, or choose their own.
6. Once the mural has dried, children can glue the Water Lily patterns onto the mural.
7. Post the completed pictures on a bulletin board labeled "Wonderful Water Lilies."

Option:
Have the children dictate words that start with w. Write one word in the center of each water lily before posting them on the mural.

Literature Link:
• *Claude Monet: Art for Children* by Ernest Raboff (Doubleday, 1968).
Show children the pictures by Monet and read to them about the artist.

Water Lily Patterns

Ww Patterns

EXTRA-SPECIAL EXTRAVAGANZA

Materials:
X-Word patterns (p. 298), crayons or markers, scissors, plastic eggs (available at arts and crafts stores near Easter), basket or other container

Preparation:
Duplicate the X-Word patterns, color, and cut out. Place one word inside each egg. Place the eggs in a basket or other container.

Directions:
1. Have the children repeat the sound of the letter "x" with you.
2. Explain that the children will be learning words that have the letter x in them.
3. Give each child a turn to remove an egg from the basket and open it. Help the children sound out the words in the eggs.
4. When all eggs have been opened, replace them in the basket and continue.

Note:
To do this activity without plastic eggs, copy the X-Word patterns and place them in a basket or container. Let each child have a turn to pick one pattern from the container.

Literature Link:
• *Rechenka's Eggs* by Patricia Polacco (Philomel, 1988). An injured goose lays marvelously colored eggs to replace the ones she's broken.

box

fox

ox

extra

x-ray

fix

six

X-Word Patterns

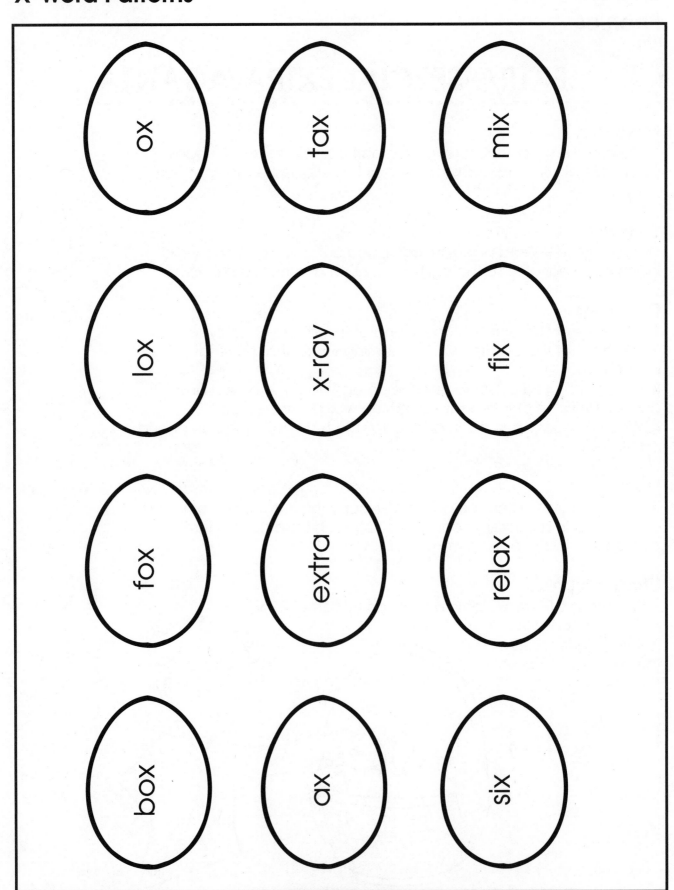

BOUNCING EGGS

. . . .

Materials:
Eggs (one per group of four children), saucepan, water, glass or jar (one per group of four children), vinegar

Preparation:
Hard boil the eggs. Place one egg in each jar.

Directions:
1. Divide the children into groups of four and give each group one egg in a jar.
2. Pour enough vinegar into each jar to cover the egg.
3. Change the vinegar each day for three days.
4. On the fourth day, remove the eggs and have the children take turns dropping the eggs on a table. The eggs will bounce.
5. Explain that there are certain minerals in eggshells. These minerals make the eggshells hard. The vinegar removes the minerals and makes the shells soft.

Literature Link:
• *Eggbert, the Slightly Cracked Egg* by Tom Ross, illustrated by Rex Barron (Putnam, 1994).
A cracked egg realizes that being cracked can be something to be proud of!

BACK TO NATURAL

Materials:
Spinach leaves, saucepan with lid, water, knife (for adult use only),
eggs (one per child)

Preparation:
Hard boil the eggs.

Directions:
1. Explain that long ago people colored their clothes with dyes
made from natural items, such as plants, flowers, and leaves.
2. Give each child a handful of spinach leaves.
3. Have the children tear the leaves into small pieces.
4. Place the leaves in a pan of water.
5. Boil the spinach for a few minutes.
6. Add the eggs, remove the pan from the heat, and cover the pan.
7. Let the eggs soak in the water for half an hour. The eggshells will
turn green!
8. Give each child a "spinach egg" to take home.

Option:
Color eggs using other natural dyes. Soak eggs in chopped red
cabbage and water, crushed strawberries or blueberries and water, or
grated orange or lemon peel and water.

Literature Link:
• *The Amazing Egg Book* by Margaret Griffin and Deborah Seed,
illustrated by Linda Hendry
(Addison-Wesley, 1989).
This book discusses where
eggs come from, what
functions they serve,
and how they can be
used for food
or decoration.

BUTTERFLY, BUTTERFLY

Materials:
Butterfly patterns (p. 303), Butterfly Math Rhyme (pp. 304-305), crayons or markers, scissors, envelopes (one per child)

Preparation:
Duplicate the Butterfly patterns and Butterfly Math Rhyme for each child.

Directions:
1. Give each child a copy of the Butterfly patterns to color and cut out.
2. Teach the children the Butterfly Math Rhyme. Children can use the Butterfly patterns to count with during the rhyme.
3. Place the Butterfly Math Rhyme and the Butterfly patterns in envelopes for the children to take home. They can continue their math practice with their families.

Option:
Perform this counting song for other classes or for parents.

Literature Link:
• *Swallowtail Butterflies* by Jane Dallinger and Cynthia Overbeck (Lerner, 1982).
Share the color photographs with students, and read them some of the many interesting facts.

Butterfly Patterns

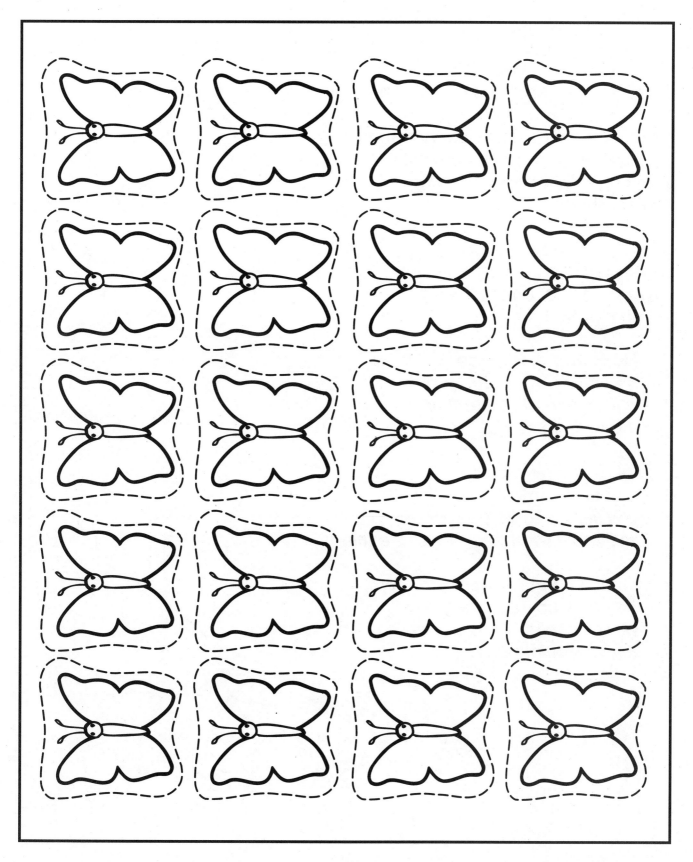

Butterfly Math Rhyme (1-9)

(This rhyme can be sung to the tune of "Take Me Out to the Ball Game")

I went out to the meadow,
I went out to a park.
I saw a flurry of colored wings.
I didn't know what to make of the things.

But I followed quickly behind them,
As they flew up, up, and away.
I saw one, two, three butterflies
On this springtime day.

I went out to the meadow,
I went out to a park.
I saw a flurry of colored wings.
I didn't know what to make of the things.

But I followed quickly behind them,
As they flew up, up, and away.
I saw four, five, six butterflies
On this springtime day.

I went out to the meadow,
I went out to a park.
I saw a flurry of colored wings.
I didn't know what to make of the things.

But I followed quickly behind them,
As they flew up, up, and away.
I saw seven, eight, nine butterflies
On this springtime day.

Butterfly Math Rhyme (10-20)

I went out to the meadow,
I went out to a park.
I saw a flurry of colored wings.
I didn't know what to make of the things.

But I followed quickly behind them,
As they flew up, up, and away.
I saw ten, eleven, twelve butterflies
On this springtime day.

I went out to the meadow,
I went out to a park.
I saw a flurry of colored wings.
I didn't know what to make of the things.

But I followed quickly behind them,
As they flew up, up, and away.
I saw thirteen, fourteen, fifteen butterflies
On this springtime day.

I went out to the meadow,
I went out to a park.
I saw a flurry of colored wings.
I didn't know what to make of the things.

But I followed quickly behind them,
As they flew up, up, and away.
I saw sixteen, seventeen, eighteen butterflies
On this springtime day.

I went out to the meadow,
I went out to a park.
I saw a flurry of colored wings.
I didn't know what to make of the things.

But I followed quickly behind them,
As they flew up, up, and away.
I saw nineteen and twenty butterflies
On this springtime day. Yea!

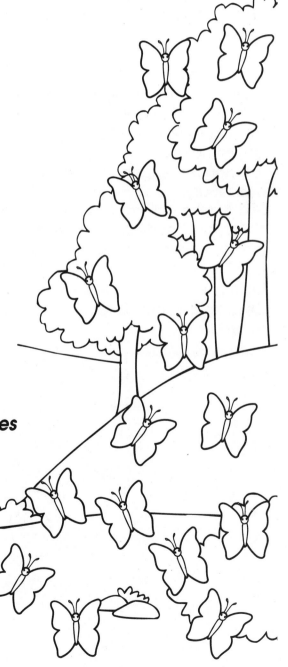

EGGSHELL TREASURES

Materials:
Uncooked eggs (one per child), small paper cups (one per child), tempera paint, small paintbrushes, glue, glitter, sequins, sticky stars, pin (for teacher use only), water

Preparation:
None.

Directions:
1. Give each child an egg and a paper cup.
2. Make a small hole at each end of each egg with a pin.
3. Demonstrate how to blow into one hole in an egg so that the insides empty into the cup below. (If needed, enlarge the holes.)
4. When the eggs have been emptied, rinse them gently under water and let dry.
5. Have the children paint the eggshells and let them dry.
6. Provide assorted decorations (glitter, sequins, sticky stars) for children to glue to their painted eggshells.

Option:
Children can cut pictures from magazines to glue to their painted eggshells.

ROLLER FLOWERS

Materials:
White butcher paper, scissors, paint in squirt bottles, foam rollers or large paintbrushes, felt pen, crayons or pencils

Preparation:
Make work stations on classroom tables. Cut large pieces of butcher paper for four children to work on at once.

Directions:
1. Give each child a sponge roller or large brush.
2. Squirt different colors of paint directly onto the paper. Move the paint bottle around so thin lines of paint form patterns on the paper.
3. The children can use their rollers or brushes to smear the paint over the entire paper. (Add more paint if needed.)
4. Let the papers dry, then turn them paint-side down. The children can take turns drawing large flower outlines on the paper.
5. Cut out the flowers. Print each child's name on the back of his or her flower.
6. Tape the flowers in a row to make a kaleidoscopic flower garden.

RABBIT RACES

Materials:
Rabbit pattern (p. 309), scissors, yarn, crayons or markers, two small chairs, hole punch, tape

Preparation:
Duplicate a copy of the Rabbit pattern for each child. Punch a hole at the top of the patterns (as shown). Cut two long pieces of yarn and tape the pieces of yarn across two chairs.

Directions:
1. Give each child a copy of the Rabbit pattern to color and cut out.
2. Explain that the children will be having rabbit races. Two children at a time will race their rabbits along the strings. Place the rabbits on the strings by removing one end of the tape, sliding one rabbit onto each piece of yarn, then reattaching.
3. Two additional children should watch to make sure the rabbit racers follow the rules: only one hand is used to move a rabbit; a rabbit has to travel the length of the yarn twice.
4. The rest of the children can watch and clap. The rabbit racer who finishes first is the winner, but allow both rabbits to finish the race.
5. Give each child a turn to race his or her rabbit.
6. At the end of the rabbit races, post the rabbits on a "Rabbit Racers" bulletin board.

Literature Link:
• *Rabbit* by Mark Evans (Dorling Kindersley, 1992).
This is an informative ASPCA guide.

Rabbit Pattern

DOES A COW GO "PEEP"?

Materials:
Animal Sound patterns (p. 311), scissors, glue, flannel, flannel board, crayons or markers

Preparation:
Duplicate a copy of the Animal Sound patterns to color, cut out, and use on a flannel board. Attach a small piece of flannel to the back of each pattern.

Directions:
1. Explain that animals have their own special languages. Each animal makes a special sound. Ask the children to think of different animals and the sounds they make.
2. Teach the children The Mixed-Up Animal Rhyme. As you say the names of the animals, place each animal pattern on the flannel board.

> ### The Mixed-Up Animal Rhyme
> *A sheep and a chick and an old brown cow,*
> *Got together on the farm and, wow, somehow...*
> *All their sounds got all mixed up,*
> *And the worried farmer said, "Hey, what's up?"*

3. Place the word balloons on the flannel board as you read the third line, with the wrong sound coming from each animal. Add the farmer and his word balloon when you read the last line.
4. Let the children help you place the right word balloon with each animal.

Option:
Duplicate the rhyme and patterns to send home with the children.

Literature Link:
• *Moo, Baa, La, La, La* by Sandra Boynton (Little Simon, 1982). This board book of different animals includes singing pigs!

Animal Sound Patterns

**Farm Animals
Science**

EXAMINE AN EGG!

Materials:
Egg pattern (p. 313), one uncooked egg for every four children, one shallow tray for each egg, yellow crayons, tape

Preparation:
Duplicate a copy of the Egg pattern for each child. Enlarge one copy of the pattern and color the yolk yellow. Tape the pattern on a wall.

Directions:
1. Place shallow trays on tables. Have four children sit by each tray. Place a raw egg in each tray.
2. Have the children observe the egg. Explain that the hard outer shell protects a baby chicken while it is developing inside. The shell also keeps out harmful germs.
3. Crack each of the eggs. Leave the two eggshell halves in the trays. Point to the enlarged pattern on the wall and explain that this is what the children are seeing.
4. Discuss the different parts of the egg and point to the parts on the pattern. The children can find:
• The large yellow part of the egg called the yolk. The yolk supplies food for the chick.
• The small white patch on the yolk called the *ovum*. Inside the ovum, the baby chick first begins to develop.
• The thick white rope on either end of the yolk called the *chalaza* (ka-lā-za). It holds the yolk in place.
• The clear jelly-like substance around the yolk called the *albumen* or egg white. It also provides food for the developing chick.
• The rounded end of the broken eggshell, where an air pocket will be. This is where the chick's head develops. When the chick is ready to hatch, it pokes its beak into this air pocket and breathes.

Option:
Give each child a copy of the Egg pattern. The children can color the yolks yellow and take the patterns home.

Egg Pattern

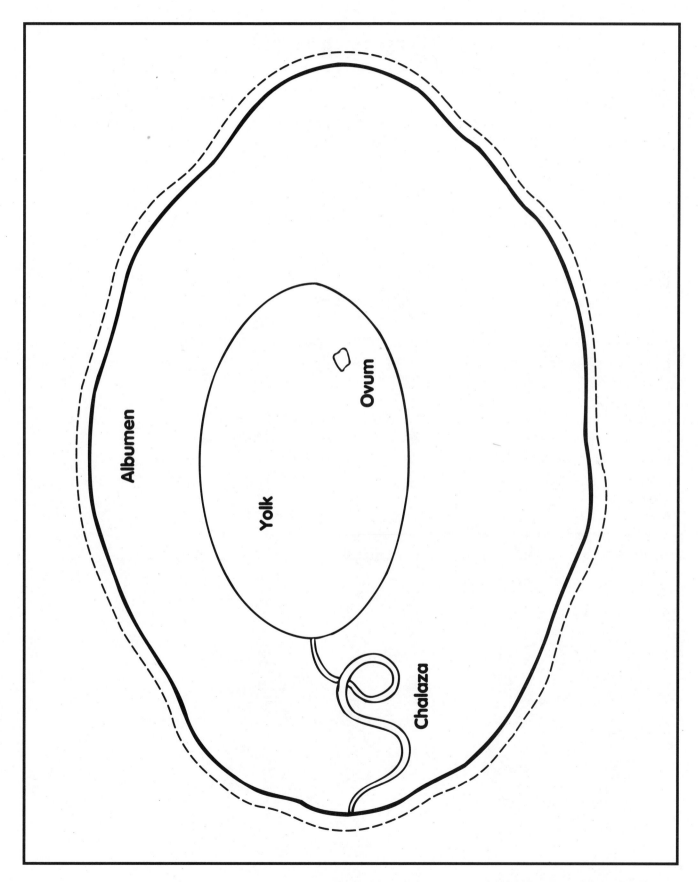

Albumen

Yolk

Ovum

Chalaza

CHICK MATH

Materials:
Chick and Nest patterns (p. 317), Chick Math Rhyme (pp. 315-316), crayons or markers, scissors, paper plates (1 1/2 per child), glue, stapler

Preparation:
Duplicate the Chick and Nest patterns and Chick Math Rhyme for each child.

Directions:
1. Give each child a copy of the Chick patterns to color and cut out.
2. Show children how to make paper plate pockets by stapling half of a paper plate onto a full paper plate (as shown).
3. Children can glue their Nest patterns to the front of the paper plate pockets.
4. Have the children place their chicks in their paper plate pockets.
5. As you read the Chick Math Rhyme, the children can take one chick at a time from the nest.

Literature Link:
• *The Wonderful Egg* by G. Warren Schloat, Jr. (Scribner's, 1952). This black and white photograph book answers almost every possible question about chickens and eggs!

Chick Math Rhyme (10-5)

Ten little chicks are sleeping on the farm.
It's a hot day and the chicks are warm.
One little chick hops out of the nest.
Now there are . . . (nine) chickies taking a rest.

Nine little chicks are sleeping on the farm.
It's a hot day and the chicks are warm.
One little chick hops out of the nest.
Now there are . . . (eight) chickies taking a rest.

Eight little chicks are sleeping on the farm.
It's a hot day and the chicks are warm.
One little chick hops out of the nest.
Now there are . . . (seven) chickies taking a rest.

Seven little chicks are sleeping on the farm.
It's a hot day and the chicks are warm.
One little chick hops out of the nest.
Now there are . . . (six) chickies taking a rest.

Six little chicks are sleeping on the farm.
It's a hot day and the chicks are warm.
One little chick hops out of the nest.
Now there are . . . (five) chickies taking a rest.

Chick Math Rhyme (5-0)

Five little chicks are sleeping on the farm.
It's a hot day and the chicks are warm.
One little chick hops out of the nest.
Now there are . . . (four) chickies taking a rest.

Four little chicks are sleeping on the farm.
It's a hot day and the chicks are warm.
One little chick hops out of the nest.
Now there are . . . (three) chickies taking a rest.

Three little chicks are sleeping on the farm.
It's a hot day and the chicks are warm.
One little chick hops out of the nest.
Now there are . . . (two) chickies taking a rest.

Two little chicks are sleeping on the farm.
It's a hot day and the chicks are warm.
One little chick hops out of the nest.
Now there is . . . (one) chickie taking a rest.

One little chick is sleeping on the farm.
It's a hot day and the chick is warm.
That little chick hops out of the nest.
Now there are . . . (no) chickies taking a rest.

No little chicks are feeling awfully warm.
It's too hot a day to sit outside on the farm.
The pigs are staying cool by splashing in the mud.
The cows are in the shade, just chewing on their cud.
The horses and the sheep are underneath the trees,
And nobody's moving except the flies and the bees.

Chick and Nest Patterns

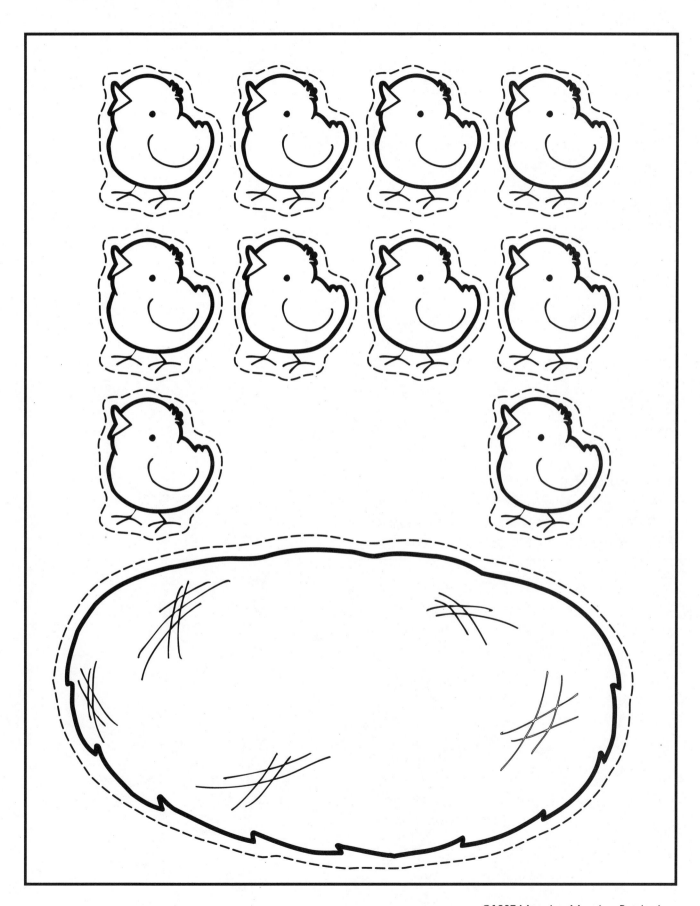

FLUFFY CHICKS

Materials:
Yellow cotton balls (available at many art and craft stores), glue, orange construction paper, scissors

Preparation:
None.

Directions:
1. Give each child yellow cotton balls to glue together to form round, fluffy shapes. These will be the bodies of the chicks. The children can decide how big or small to make their chicks.
2. Give each child a piece of orange paper to use to cut out a beak.
3. Children can glue the beaks to their chicks.

Option:
Let children carefully color black eyes on the cotton balls with thin-tipped markers.

Literature Link:
• *Farm Babies* by Russell Freedman (Holiday House, 1981). This nonfiction book answers such questions as, "How do mother hens call their chicks?"

COW COUNTING

Materials:
Cow pattern (p. 320), clothesline, pair of dice, scissors, tape, white construction paper, brown crayons, clothespins (one per child), two chairs

Preparation:
Duplicate a copy of the Cow pattern for each child. Suspend a piece of clothesline between two chairs. Clip the clothespins across the clothesline.

Directions:
1. Give each child a copy of the Cow pattern to color and cut out.
2. Have the children clip their paper cows to the clothesline.
3. Have the children observe the cows and count how many cows are in the herd.
4. Teach the children The Cow Jingle. Clap to establish a rhythm.

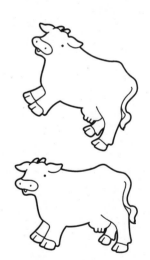

> ### The Cow Jingle
> *I went to the market to buy some brown cows.*
> *I looked at the chickens, I looked at the sows.*
> *I looked at the piglets and almost forgot*
> *Those brown spotted cows that needed to be bought!*

5. Ask a child the following question: "How many cows are you going to buy?"
6. This child can roll the dice and move that number of cows into a separate group on the line.
7. Ask the question, "How many cows did you leave behind?" The children can count the number of cows that were not bought.
8. Repeat The Cow Jingle. Continue until all children have had a turn to buy cows.

Literature Link:
• *George Washington's Cows* by David Small (Farrar, 1994).
This silly, rhyming story is about cows that live with Washington.

Cow Pattern

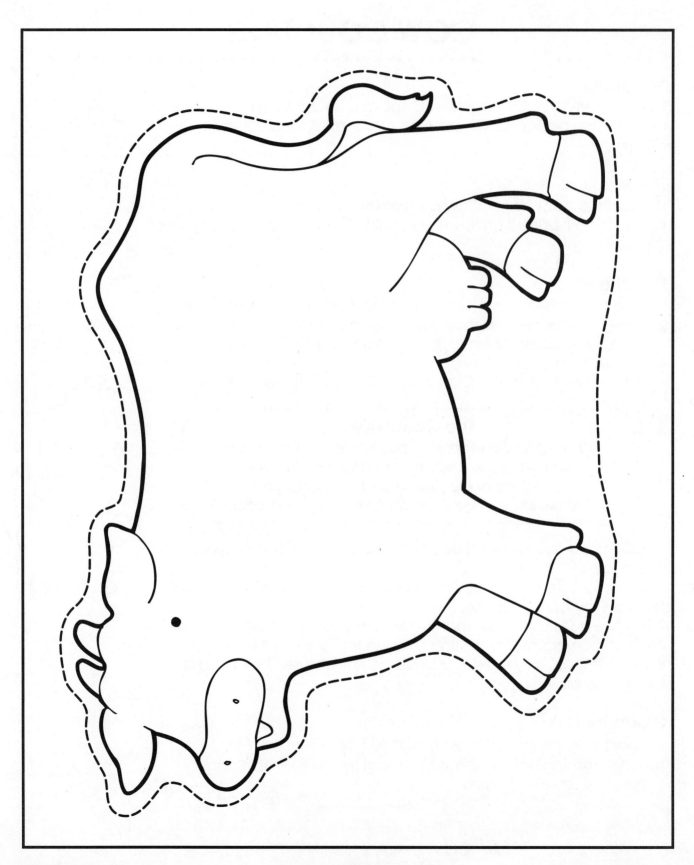

Chapter Nine
Summer and Oceans

SUMMERTIME ANIMAL CHANT

Materials:
Summertime Animal Chant (p. 323)

Preparation:
Duplicate a copy of the Summertime Animal Chant for each child.

Summer Animal Facts:
- Arctic hares have white fur in the winter to blend in with the snow. They turn brown when the snow melts because they no longer need the white camouflage for protection.
- Dogs pant because they cannot sweat to stay cool.
- Elephants spray themselves with their trunks to cool down. They can give themselves water or mud baths this way. Elephants also wave their ears back and forth to cool down.
- Camels can stand very hot weather. They don't have much fat under their skin to store heat.
- Armadillos breathe fast, flop on their sides, and pant to stay cool.

Directions:
1. Explain that different animals have different ways of coping with hot summer weather. Some animals, like dogs, pant. Other animals have a variety of ways of beating the heat!
2. Read some of the animal facts to the children.
3. Teach the children the Summertime Animal Chant. Clap to establish a rhythm.

Literature Links:
- *African Elephants: Giants of the Land* by Dorothy Hinshaw Patent, photographs by Oria Douglas-Hamilton (Holiday House, 1991).
This book's many facts are accompanied by amazing photos.
- *Warm-Blooded Animals* by Maurice Burton (Orbis, 1985).
Many animals, including elephants, camels, armadillos, and hares, are featured.

Summertime Animal Chant

Buffaloes shed and goats climb high.
Butterflies flap their wings and fly,
And arctic hares, but not the bears,
Change their white fur to brown.

Armadillos flop onto their sides.
Water cools the hippos' hides,
And arctic hares, but not the bears,
Change their white fur to brown.

Tigers chill out in the water.
Foxes' fur thins as it gets hotter,
And arctic hares, but not the bears,
Change their white fur to brown.

Elephants shower their dusty backs.
Dogs pant hard, and cats take naps,
And arctic hares, but not the bears,
Change their white fur to brown.

Camels turn their fat to water.
Sea foam cools the swimming otters,
And arctic hares, but not the bears,
Change their white fur to brown.

YES AND NO

· ·

Materials:
"Yes and No" patterns, (p. 325), scissors

Preparation:
Duplicate and cut apart enough "Yes and No" patterns
for each child to have a set.

> What do you say when you eat something you like?

Directions:
1. Have the children repeat the sound of the letter "y" with you.
Ask questions that can be answered with words that start with "y,"
for example:
- "What do you say when you eat something you like?" (Yum!)
- "What's the name of the round toy with the long string?" (yo-yo)
- "What color is the center of an egg?" (yellow)
- "What is the center of an egg called?" (yolk)
- "What are you called if you are not old?" (young)

> What color is the center of an egg?

2. Give each child a "yes" pattern and a "no" pattern. Ask the children
to tell you which one begins with the letter "y."
3. Explain that you will ask a variety of questions and the children will
answer them by holding up their "yes" or "no" cards.
4. Ask questions that relate to summer, for example:
- "Do you like to swim in the summer?"
- "Do you wear heavy jackets during the summer?"
- "Is it hotter during the summer than the rest of the year?"

> What is the center of an egg called?

5. Let the children take their "yes" and "no" cards home. Encourage
the children to have someone at their home ask them "yes" and "no"
questions. Send a note home to the parents explaining that they should
ask their children "yes" or "no" questions and let the children hold up the
appropriate card.

> What's the name of the round toy with the long string?

Literature Link:
- *Yo! Yes?*
by Chris Raschka
(Orchard, 1993).
Two boys meet on the
street and decide to
become friends.

YES

NO

YES

NO

Yy Patterns

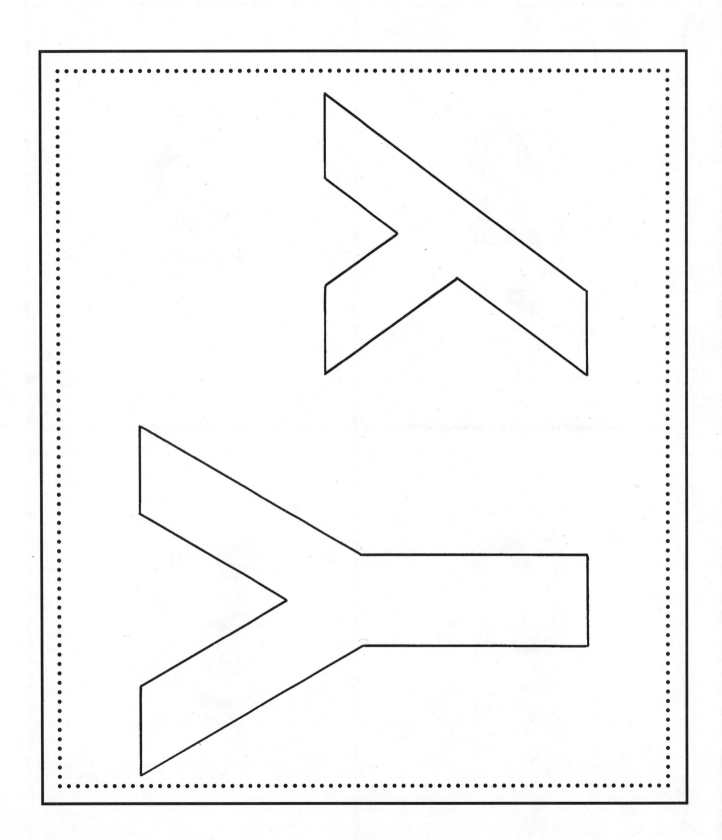

THE ZIGZAG "Z"

Materials:
"Zz" patterns (p. 328), felt pens, pipe cleaners. scissors

Preparation:
Duplicate a copy of the "Zz" patterns for each child. Cut enough pipe cleaners in half for each child to have one half.

Directions:
1. Have children repeat the sound of the letter "z" with you.
2. Give each child a copy of the "Zz" patterns and a pipe cleaner half.
3. Have the children coil their pipe cleaners around their fingers. The pipe cleaners will represent newly-hatched caterpillars.
4. Have the children place their caterpillars at the top left of their papers. Teach the children the "Zigzag Chant." As the children say the chant, they can move their caterpillars along the top line of the Zs, zigzag them down the slanted line, then zoom to the end.

Zigzag Chant
(to the tune of "The Eency, Weency Spider")
The tiny, hungry caterpillar crawled across the vine.
He zigzagged down to see what he could find.
He looked to the left, then he looked to the right.
Then he yelled out "Zounds!" when he found something to bite!

Literature Link:
• *The Z Was Zapped* by Chris Van Allsburg (Houghton Mifflin, 1987). The letters of the alphabet are struck by mishap in this illustrated play in 26 one-page acts.

SUMMER SUNDIAL

Materials:
Rhino Clock pattern (p. 241), paper plates (one per child), clay,
Popsicle sticks or straws (one per child), paste or glue, scissors, watch

Preparation:
Duplicate a copy of the Rhino Clock pattern for each child.

Directions:
1. Give each child a copy of the Rhino Clock pattern to cut
out and glue to a paper plate.
2. Provide bits of clay for each child to mold into a small ball.
3. Have each child place the clay in the center of his or her clock.
4. Demonstrate how to anchor a straw or Popsicle stick in the clay.
5. Have the children take their sundials outside and place them on the
ground. Help children position the sundials to show the correct time.
6. Have the children observe the shadows that the sun creates on their
paper plates.
7. Take the children outside a few times during the day and have them
see if the shadows have moved.

Literature Link:
• *Our Planet Earth* by Robert Estalella, illustrated by Marcel Socias
(Barron's, 1994).
This resource includes directions for making a sundial.

MOTH MATH

. . . .

Materials:
Moth and Butterfly patterns (p. 331), Ten Little Insects rhyme (pp. 332-333), crayons or felt pens, scissors, envelopes (one per child)

Preparation:
Duplicate a copy of the patterns and the rhyme for each child.

Butterfly and Moth Facts:
- Butterflies have thin antennae and thin bodies.
- Moths have feathery antennae and fat, furry bodies.
- There are more types of moths than butterflies.
- Moths usually fly at night and butterflies fly during the day.
- Butterflies and moths that live in temperate climates tend to have a wingspan of between two and six centimeters. Those that live in the tropics can have a span of up to 20 centimeters!

Directions:
1. Discuss the differences between butterflies and moths and read some of the facts listed above.
2. Give each child a copy of the Moth and Butterfly patterns to color and cut out. Point out which of the patterns are moths and which are butterflies. (The moths are fat with furry bodies.)
3. Have the children count the number of moths and butterflies. (There are five moths and five butterflies.)
4. Have the children line up their five moths and five butterflies.
5. Read the Ten Little Insects rhyme and let the children move the patterns out of the lines as you read each verse.
6. Let the children take home their patterns and a copy of the rhyme in envelopes. They can practice counting at home.

Literature Link:
- *The Fascinating World of Butterflies and Moths* by Angels Julivert (Barron's, 1991). This resource is filled with many interesting facts and beautiful illustrations.

Moth and Butterfly Patterns

Ten Little Insects (10-5)

Ten little insects were flying in the sky.
Five were moths, and five were butterflies.
One little moth flew off far away,
But the other . . . (nine) insects decided they would stay.

Nine little insects were flying in the sky.
Four were moths, and five were butterflies.
One little butterfly flew off far away,
But the other . . . (eight) insects decided they would stay.

Eight little insects were flying in the sky.
Four were moths, and four were butterflies.
One little moth flew off far away,
But the other . . . (seven) insects decided they would stay.

Seven little insects were flying in the sky.
Three were moths, and four were butterflies.
One little butterfly flew off far away,
But the other . . . (six) insects decided they would stay.

Six little insects were flying in the sky.
Three were moths, and three were butterflies.
One little moth flew off far away,
But the other . . . (five) insects decided they would stay.

Ten Little Insects (5-0)

Five little insects were flying in the sky.
Two were moths, and three were butterflies.
One little butterfly flew off far away,
But the other . . . (four) insects decided they would stay.

Four little insects were flying in the sky.
Two were moths, and two were butterflies.
One little moth flew off far away,
But the other . . . (three) insects decided they would stay.

Three little insects were flying in the sky.
One was a moth, and two were butterflies.
One little butterfly flew off far away,
But the other . . . (two) insects decided they would stay.

Two little insects were flying in the sky.
One was a moth, and one was a butterfly.
The little white moth flew off far away,
But the other . . . (one) insect decided it would stay.

One little insect was flying in the sky.
That lonely insect was a little butterfly.
That little butterfly flew off to find a friend
And now that he's gone, this rhyme has reached the end!

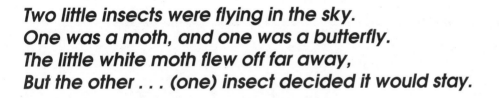

Moth Number Sets

🦋	1	🦋🦋	2
🦋🦋🦋	3	🦋🦋🦋🦋	4
🦋🦋🦋🦋🦋	5	🦋🦋🦋🦋🦋🦋	6
🦋🦋🦋🦋🦋🦋🦋	7	🦋🦋🦋🦋🦋🦋🦋🦋	8
🦋🦋🦋🦋🦋🦋🦋🦋🦋	9	🦋🦋🦋🦋🦋🦋🦋🦋🦋🦋	10

334

TAKE-HOME SHADOWS

. . . .

Materials:
Butcher paper, scissors, crayons or markers

Preparation:
Cut butcher paper into sheets that are at least as tall as your students. Cut one sheet for each child.

Directions:
1. Ask the question, "How can you take home a shadow?" Have the children brainstorm possible answers.
2. Give each child a sheet of butcher paper and a crayon or marker.
3. Pair the children up and take them outside to a flat surface.
4. Explain that the partners will be tracing each other's shadows. Have one of the partners place a sheet of butcher paper on the ground and stand so that his or her shadow appears on the paper. The other partner traces the first's shadow.
5. Have the partners switch, so every child's shadow is traced.
6. The children can color their shadows and cut them out.
7. Have children take their shadows home to share with friends and family members.

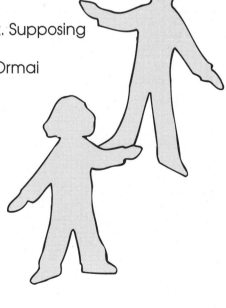

Literature Links:
• *In Shadowland* by Mitsumasa Anno (Orchard, 1988).
"Suppose there was a land of shadows," begins this book. Supposing there is one, Anno has certainly captured it!
• *Shadow Magic* by Seymour Simon, illustrated by Stella Ormai (Lothrop, 1985).
This book explains what shadows are and how they are formed.

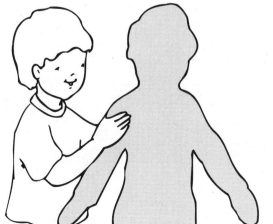

SUNSHINE ART

· ·

Materials:
White construction paper, crayons or felt pens

Preparation:
None

Directions:
1. Take children on a walk on a sunny day.
2. Have the children observe the sunlight falling on objects, such as plants, trees, the sidewalk, grass, themselves, and so on.
3. When you are back in the classroom, have the children draw something they saw on their walk that was touched by sunlight.
4. Post the finished drawings on a bulletin board labeled "Sunshine Art."

Option:
Pass out sunflower seeds to plant at home in a sunny spot. The sunflowers will keep track of the sun. They move their large heads to face the sun's warmth.

Literature Link:
• *Summer Is...* by Charlotte Zolotow, illustrated by Janet Archer (Abelard-Schuman, 1967).
"Summer is porches and cold lemonade." When summer's over, fall brings "squirrels on the rooftop." Winter means "pink skies early in the evening." And "spring is cats prowling and the green of new grass."

TRIP TO THE SEASHORE

Materials:
Seashells (available at arts and crafts stores)

Preparation:
Set the seashells out on a table.

Directions:
1. Have the children discuss trips that they have taken with their families to the seashore.
2. Take the children on an imaginary trip to the seashore. Have the children sit on the rug with their eyes closed while you describe a visit to the beach. Talk about the sound of the waves, the feel of the sand, the smell of the salt air, and the sound of sea gulls.
3. Give each child a turn to observe the seashells.

Option:
Have the children bring in seashell collections to share.

Literature Link:
• *The Seashore Book* by Charlotte Zolotow, paintings by Wendell Minor (HarperCollins, 1992).
A mother describes a trip to the seashore to her son, who has never been.

©1997 Monday Morning Books, Inc.

ROARING SHELLS

Materials:
Large spiral seashells (available from arts and crafts stores)

Preparation:
None.

Directions:
1. Give each child a turn to hold the seashell to his or her ears.
2. Ask the children to describe what they hear.
3. Explain that many people think they can hear ocean waves inside a seashell!
4. Let the children listen to the shells again.
5. Explain that what they are hearing are the sounds of echoes within the shell. Because of the shell's shape and its inside smoothness, the sounds from outside vibrate. This causes the roaring sound that people associate with waves.

Literature Link:
• *Shells* by Jennifer Coldrey (Dorling Kindersley, 1993).
This book describes the behavior, anatomy, and inner workings of assorted shelled animals.

BEACHCOMBING

Materials:
Beachcombing pattern (p. 340), pencils, crayons

Preparation:
Duplicate a copy of the Beachcombing pattern for each child.

Directions:
1. Explain that beachcombing means walking along the beach and looking for interesting objects. Ask if any children have ever been beachcombing. If so, ask them what they found.
2. Give each child a copy of the Beachcombing pattern and a pencil. Ask the children what they would find if they went beachcombing on this beach. Identify the objects in the picture together: sand crabs, sand dollars, starfish, and seashells.
3. Have the children count the number of sand crabs, sand dollars, seashells, and starfish.
4. Let the children color in the pattern.

Option:
Duplicate the Shell patterns (p. 341) and the Beach Rhyme (p. 342). Give each child a copy of the Shell patterns to color and cut out. Read the rhyme aloud and have children place the patterns in the right order.

Literature Link:
• *The Starfish: A Treasure-chest Story* by Hilde Heyduck-Huth (Margaret K. McElderry Books, 1987).
A little girl finds a forgotten starfish and puts it in her treasure chest.

Beachcombing Pattern

Shell Patterns

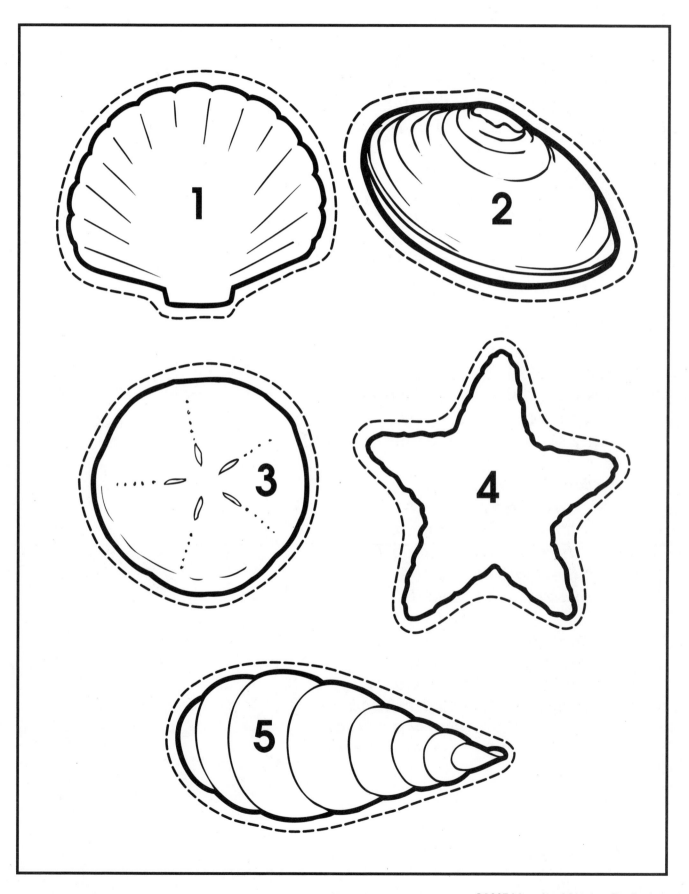

Beach Rhyme

I was walking on the beach,
A flat seashell was in my reach.
I brushed off all the bits of sand,
And took the shell home in my hand.
The shell was warm from the summer sun,
How many seashells did I have? (One!)

I was walking on the beach,
A mussel shell was in my reach.
I brushed off all the bits of sand,
And took the shell home in my hand.
The inside was a dark and inky blue.
How many shells did I have then? (Two!)

I was walking on the beach,
A sand dollar was within my reach.
I brushed off all the bits of sand,
And took the shell home in my hand.
I put my shells out for all to see.
How many shells did I have then? (Three!)

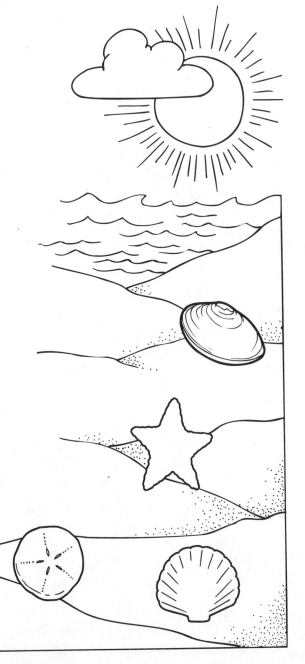

I was walking on the beach,
A starfish was within my reach.
I brushed off all the bits of sand,
And took the star home in my hand.
I lined up the shells that I adore,
How many shells did I have then? (Four!)

I was walking on the beach,
A spiral shell was within my reach.
I brushed off all the bits of sand,
And took the shell home in my hand.
My new shell looked sort of like a hive.
How many shells did I have then? (Five!)

Beach Number Sets

🐚	1	🐚🐚	2
🐚🐚🐚	3	🐚🐚🐚🐚	4
🐚🐚🐚🐚🐚	5	🐚🐚🐚🐚🐚🐚	6
🐚🐚🐚🐚🐚🐚🐚	7	🐚🐚🐚🐚🐚🐚🐚🐚	8
🐚🐚🐚🐚🐚🐚🐚🐚🐚	9	🐚🐚🐚🐚🐚🐚🐚🐚🐚🐚	10

343

OPEN UP THE TREASURE

. . . .

Materials:
Gold patterns (p. 345), Treasure Chest pattern (p. 346), Pirate Math Rhyme (pp. 347-348), crayons, scissors, envelopes (one per child), paste or glue

Preparation:
Duplicate a copy of the Gold and Treasure Chest patterns and the Pirate Math Rhyme for each child. Make one copy of the Math Rhyme for yourself.

Directions:
1. Give each child a copy of the Gold patterns to color and cut out.
2. Give each child a copy of the Treasure Chest pattern to color and glue to the back of an envelope.
3. Have the children line up their Gold patterns.
4. Read the Pirate Math Rhyme and have children place their Gold patterns into the treasure envelope as you read each verse.
5. Let the children take their Gold patterns and the Pirate Math Rhyme home in their Treasure Chest envelopes. They can use the rhymes and the patterns to continue counting practice at home.

Literature Link:
• *The Treasure of Cozy Cove* by Tony Ross (Farrar, 1989).
Two kittens are rescued from drowning by the infamous Cap'n Claws, who takes them on an adventure in search of the treasure of Cozy Cove.

Gold Patterns

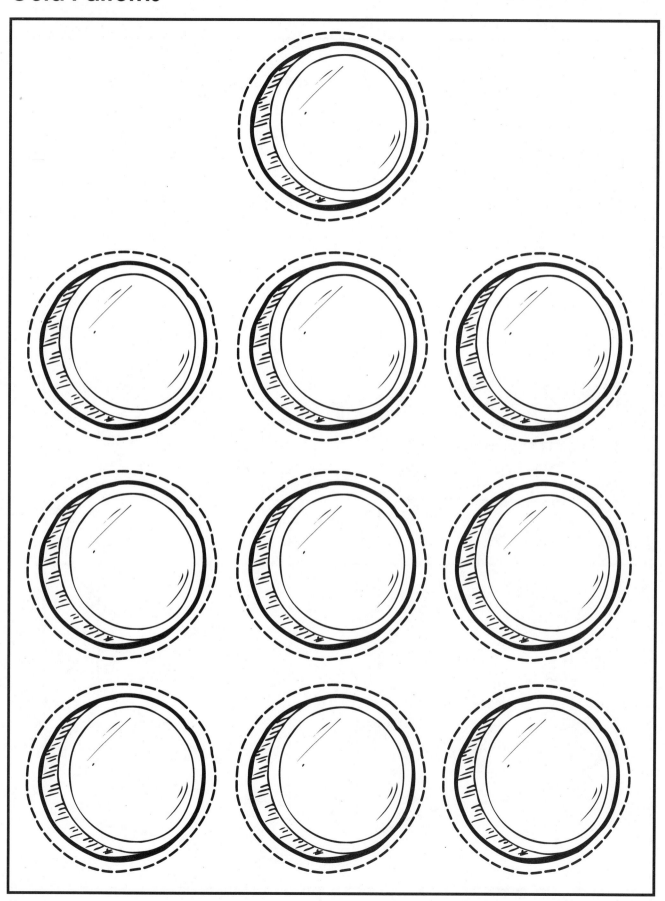

Treasure Chest Pattern

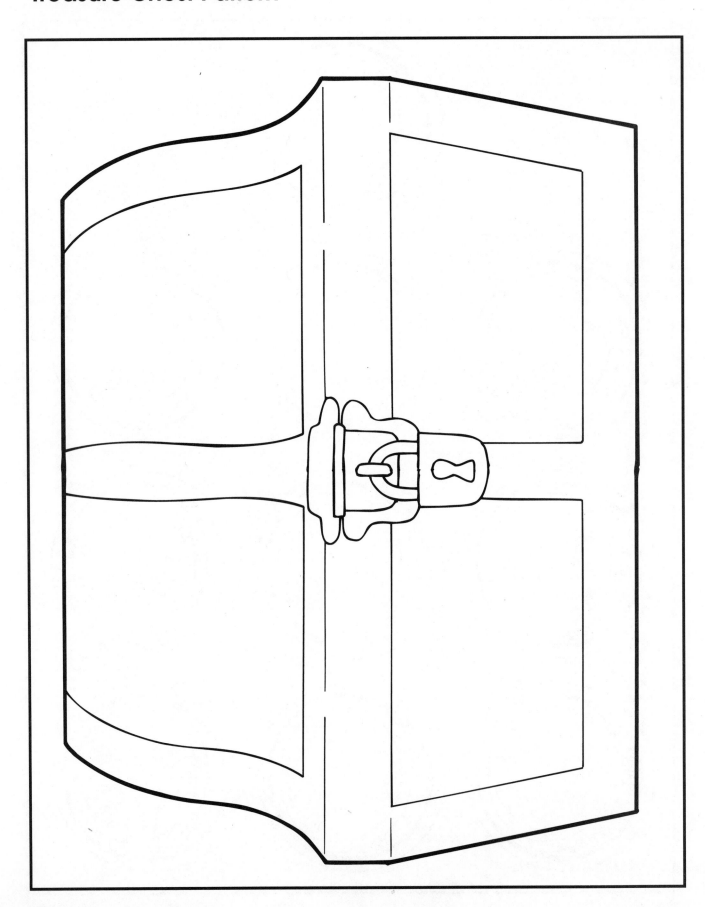

Pirate Math Rhyme (0-5)

Down in the ocean, a mile from land,
A pirate buried treasure under the sand.
So dive right down. Do as you're told,
And pick up one small piece of gold.
Then bring it back. Put it in your chest.
And add it up with all the rest!
(How many pieces of gold do you have? One!)

Down in the ocean, a mile from land,
A pirate buried treasure under the sand.
So dive right down. Do as you're told,
And pick up one small piece of gold.
Then bring it back. Put it in your chest.
And add it up with all the rest!
(How many pieces of gold do you have? Two!)

Down in the ocean, a mile from land,
A pirate buried treasure under the sand.
So dive right down. Do as you're told,
And pick up one small piece of gold.
Then bring it back. Put it in your chest.
And add it up with all the rest!
(How many pieces of gold do you have? Three!)

Down in the ocean, a mile from land,
A pirate buried treasure under the sand.
So dive right down. Do as you're told,
And pick up one small piece of gold.
Then bring it back. Put it in your chest.
And add it up with all the rest!
(How many pieces of gold do you have? Four!)

Down in the ocean, a mile from land,
A pirate buried treasure under the sand.
So dive right down. Do as you're told,
And pick up one small piece of gold.
Then bring it back. Put it in your chest.
And add it up with all the rest!
(How many pieces of gold do you have? Five!)

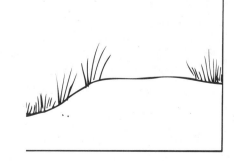

Pirate Math Rhyme (5-10)

Down in the ocean, a mile from land,
A pirate buried treasure under the sand.
So dive right down. Do as you're told,
And pick up one small piece of gold.
Then bring it back. Put it in your chest.
And add it up with all the rest!
(How many pieces of gold do you have? Six!)

Down in the ocean, a mile from land,
A pirate buried treasure under the sand.
So dive right down. Do as you're told,
And pick up one small piece of gold.
Then bring it back. Put it in your chest.
And add it up with all the rest!
(How many pieces of gold do you have? Seven!)

Down in the ocean, a mile from land,
A pirate buried treasure under the sand.
So dive right down. Do as you're told,
And pick up one small piece of gold.
Then bring it back. Put it in your chest.
And add it up with all the rest!
(How many pieces of gold do you have? Eight!)

Down in the ocean, a mile from land,
A pirate buried treasure under the sand.
So dive right down. Do as you're told,
And pick up one small piece of gold.
Then bring it back. Put it in your chest.
And add it up with all the rest!
(How many pieces of gold do you have? Nine!)

Down in the ocean, a mile from land,
A pirate buried treasure under the sand.
So dive right down. Do as you're told,
And pick up one small piece of gold.
Then bring it back. Put it in your chest.
And add it up with all the rest!
(How many pieces of gold do you have? Ten!)

Treasure Number Sets

⊙	1	⊙⊙	2
⊙⊙⊙	3	⊙⊙⊙⊙	4
⊙⊙⊙⊙⊙	5	⊙⊙⊙⊙⊙⊙	6
⊙⊙⊙⊙⊙⊙⊙	7	⊙⊙⊙⊙⊙⊙⊙⊙	8
⊙⊙⊙⊙⊙⊙⊙⊙⊙	9	⊙⊙⊙⊙⊙⊙⊙⊙⊙⊙	10

CLASSROOM CORAL REEFS

. . . .

Materials:
Coral patterns (p. 351), tape, clay, paper plates (one per child)

Preparation:
Duplicate a copy of the Coral patterns for each child.

Coral Facts:
- Coral are tiny sea animals that live in the ocean.
- Coral build skeletons around themselves for protection.
- Coral reefs are made of millions and millions of coral cups joined together.
- Coral come in many shapes and colors.

Directions:
1. Give each child a copy of the Coral patterns. Have the children observe the many different shapes in which coral can grow.
2. Make a classroom coral reef. Give each child a paper plate and colored clay. Have the children mold the clay to resemble some of the coral pictures.
3. When a piece of coral has been made, the child can place it onto a paper plate.
4. Display the coral on a table labeled "A Coral Reef: A Beautiful Underwater Garden!"

Literature Links:
- *The Underwater World of the Coral Reef* by Ann McGovern (Four Winds Press, 1976).
This resource includes many color photographs of different types of coral.
- *A Walk on the Great Barrier Reef* by Caroline Arnold (Carolrhoda Books, 1988).
This resource describes the fascinating plants and animals inhabiting the Great Barrier Reef.

Coral Patterns

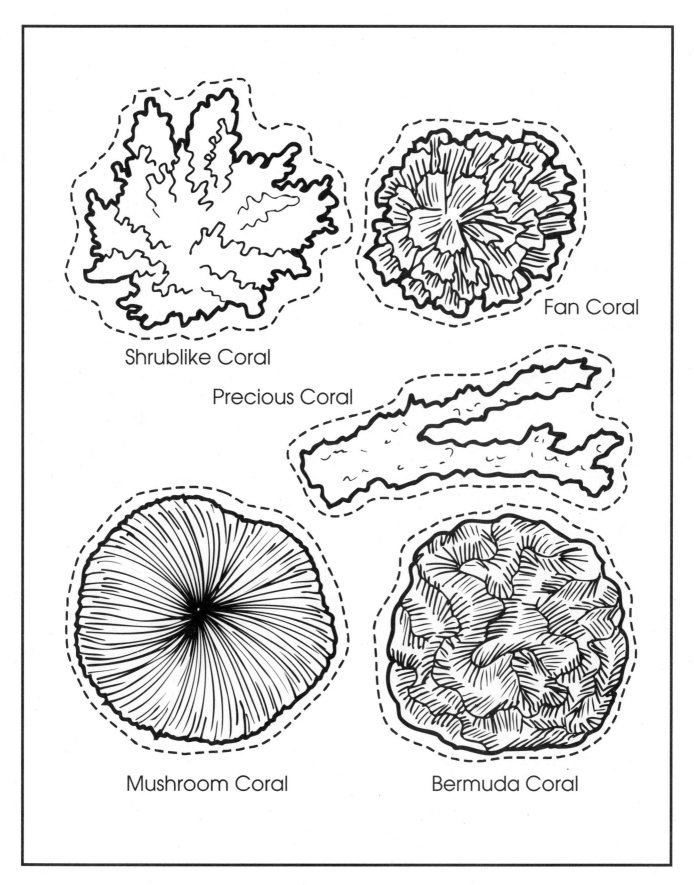

Shrublike Coral

Fan Coral

Precious Coral

Mushroom Coral

Bermuda Coral

351

MAKE A MONDAY MORNING CONNECTION

Alphabet Connections
Grades PreK-1, 352 pp., MM 1969
Fun-to-use, classroom-tested projects connect the alphabet with literature, science, and math. Adorable animal characters such as Bobby Bear are featured in activities for singing, drawing, writing, phonics, cooking, and more. Take-home pages and animal mask patterns are included.

Reading Connections
Grades PreK-1, 336 pp., MM 2026
Teach alphabet letter recognition with activities, original poems, art projects, puzzles, and favorite storybook characters such as Curious George. Make a phonics connection with mini-books and stories that build sound skills and word recognition.

Preschool Connections
Grades PreK-K, 352 pp., MM 1993
Each of the twelve units features a literature-linked art project, a fanciful retold story such as "Ruby Socks & The Three Chairs," discovery activities, dramatic play, new songs to old tunes, patterns, and more.

Storybook Connections
Grades PreK-1, 320 pp., MM 1999
These fairy-tale activities from A to Z take you through the curriculum: arts and crafts, dramatic play, literature links, marvelous math, setting the stage, story summaries, super science, and more. Fairy tales include Beauty and the Beast, Cinderella, Rapunzel, and Thumbelina.